Happy

WHY DO THEY ALWAYS SHOUT?

MEMOIRS OF A TIRED DAD
ADAM GLENNON

For Babe, Becca, and the Boys. There wouldn't be a book to write without you... so thanks xxx

(And thanks for all the editing, Wife, because there definitely wouldn't be a book without your brutal input, ahem... constructive feedback.)

First, a few thoughts from The Wife...

When the man I met, who I would later marry, told me he was embarking upon a career in writing, to say I was sceptical is an understatement.

We laugh now. After my track record of relationships with men who were, let me think of the right word... unsuitable, I had planned that anybody new in my life would need to wear a suit to work, drive a flashy car and leave me alone for the majority of the time.

What I actually got was a mature student with a dream to write and not a pot to piss in.

Our first date went something like this...

'What are you planning to study at university?'

'Well, mental health nursing is the route I'm on at the moment,'

Oh, OK. Not quite a business suit and flashy car but professional, stable, good career prospects. I'm listening...

'Nice!'

'Actually, I've decided I was following that route for the wrong reasons. I want to write. So I'm applying for a BA in Creative Writing. It's not about having a job at the end of it, it's about creativity and following your heart.'

Cue me drinking too much rum, topped up with white wine and puking over a wall while he mopped vomit out of my hair. Then put me to bed with a bowl just in case. Thankfully I had nothing left!

It might not have been part of my plan but I'm glad I took a chance on love. That's something we say to each other now and again when we're being soppy. I could see how driven he was.

His flair for telling hilarious, relatable stories unfolded and a chance blog recounting the home birth of our first son captured its essence beautifully. And the journey of documenting parenthood commenced.

Adam naturally communicates the struggles of raising smalls and I'm sure you'll relate to the tales shared in **Why Do They Always Shout?** Often, our days haven't felt light-hearted.

There have been tears and despondency with sleep deprivation at the core of our family for more than 6 years now. But, Adam has managed to encapsulate our history so that, looking back on even the darkest of days, I can smile with a warm heart knowing we did our best.

And, as parents, that's all we can do.

Enjoy.

The Wife

Thoughts from the Tired Dad...

It's a fair question, isn't it? I mean, why do they always shout? Why does every demand from their jam-stained, crumb-infested mouth need to be expressed by shouting it at us? It's not like we shout at them... well, of course we shout at them a little bit because how else are they supposed to hear and follow our very clear and vital demands? I mean instructions.

You know what, I'm tired! I'm a tired dad. Fed up. And yet I remain motivated to understand these adorable children of mine. It's become a little compulsion - a need to know *why-they-are-how-they-are* without accepting any blame whatsoever.

And it appears the only way I can find logic within the madness is to write about it. To shine a light on the challenges we all face as parents, husbands and wives, but do it with a bit of humour. No tips. No advice. Just shared experiences that will occasionally make you nod your head in agreement and at other times laugh along at the absurdity of it all!

Parenting was definitely easier years ago, wasn't it?

Our parents owned the word no. It just came so easily to them. When I say no to my boys they want to know why. A full-blown conversation is required to understand the complexities of my answer.

Do I really need to explain why it's not normal to eat your own body weight in Prawn Cocktail crisps before breakfast? Why we can't go swimming ten minutes before bed or why it's not cool to point out when someone has a double chin!

We do laugh a lot though. I'd go mad if I couldn't find the joy in things. That's why I document our experiences. It's a way to reach out to other parents in solidarity. I wanted to believe we weren't alone. In fact, I *needed* to know that other parents felt the same as we do.

And as it turns out, we're not alone.

I found you.

Worn-out mums with paint-splattered blouses wandering around the supermarket aisles with upside-down lists and an arm-scratching sugar-craving addiction for cake. Fellow dads, blurry-eyed and grey-faced pushing empty swings while their kids wait impatiently on the roundabout with their new best mate who apparently has a really cool bedroom with a swing attached to the ceiling!

I found you.

And now I know we aren't the only ones holding tightly to that beautiful and possibly naive thought... this too... shall pass!

Right, go and empty the dishwasher for the one hundredth time today. Throw some snacks in the general direction of those wonderful children of yours and close the door. Put a chair behind it. Make a brew. Put your feet up and take ten minutes for yourself while you read on for a chapter or two.

You deserve it. You're doing a fantastic job!

Tired Dad

PS. Plus we have a teenager to deal with as well. Sympathise!

Home birth... Seriously?

'Let me get this straight,' I say. 'You want to have the baby at home?'

'Yes.' The Wife replies.

Seven months pregnant and we're suddenly transported back to the 1930s.

'In a, what did you call it, a birthing pool?'

'Mmmhmm.'

I can tell she's geared up for this. Strange magazines I've never seen before have appeared on the table. Earthy-looking women are holding naked babies on the front cover. The Wife looks determined and clean. She's probably been preparing for this conversation for weeks. This is not a discussion, it's an ambush!

'It's clearly a paddling pool,' I point out.

'It's not a paddling pool.'

She thrusts her phone into my face. There's a large inflatable paddling pool with Birthing Pool written on the side.

'And we're supposed to blow this up and fill it with water just before you give birth at home right? How would that even work?'

'Don't worry about the details,' she says.

'Don't worry about the details. Do you even know me?'

She flicks through one of the magazines as if that's that. End of conversation. Doesn't she know every home birth ends in death?!

'But what about the mess? The baby could get stuck. What happens if you die, Babe? Why do you want to die?'

I'm not 100% sure what the expression on her face means. It's like a mixture of sympathy, boredom and pity. Or she thinks I'm an idiot which is a bit harsh. My mind is bombarded with hundreds of images of home birth scenes from films.

They all involve blood!

Bloody rags. Bloody hands. Smears of blood on cheeks. Boiling water. Lots of screaming. And, for reasons I can't explain, there's an elderly Irish woman in a cardigan making cups of tea and shoving

8

me towards the door before thrusting a bottle of whiskey into my hand and telling me to "Feck off."

Not once in seven months of pregnancy has she mentioned home birth. I consider myself an alternative thinker. I disbelieve everything the government says. Mainstream media's a joke. There's no desire from the pharmaceutical industry to cure disease. Mars Bars are smaller. Artificial sweeteners have ruined every fizzy drink and I most definitely believe in BigFoot.

And yet having our baby at home, in a birthing pool, is the most preposterous thing I've ever heard in my life. And that's coming from someone who has never, EVER said the word preposterous out loud before and hopefully never will again!

'Think about every film you've ever seen, Babe. No woman survives a home birth.'

'That's just patriarchy.'

'Ay?'

'The curse of Eve.'

'Ay?'

'Birthing is not a medical procedure. It's a natural event.'

'Okay.'

'In your head, all you can see is me screaming, enduring hours of pain surrounded by blood-soaked towels.'

'Exactly.'

'That's your conditioning.'

'Ay?'

'Statistically, you're less likely to have complications birthing at home.'

'I'm gonna research this hippy nonsense.'

I switch on my super slow laptop. As it begins its clinking and humming routine, some insights seep into my consciousness.

- Hospitals are not fun.
- Hospitals are for the sick.
- Nobody likes hospitals.
- Hospitals smell like they're hiding something.
- Our house is nice - it's home.

- There's wine and cake here.
- I know the piss on the toilet seat is mine.

Fifteen minutes later...

Why has no one thought of this before?

'We'll have control over everything,' I say.

'Yes.'

'We could devise a relaxing playlist. Organise some mood lighting. Smelly things to create an inviting environment. Tasty treats. Maybe even a glass of organic ale?'

'And only the right people would be present. And the option of a water birth would be practically guaranteed.'

'But what happens if something goes wrong, Babe, seriously?'

The Wife wraps an arm around my neck and kisses me softly on the cheek.

'This is a lot to take in. Let's have a break,' she says.

'What do you want to do?'

'Erm, sex?'

'No.'

'Pub?'

'No'

'Netflix?'

'Good husband.'

I turn off the laptop and get comfy on the sofa.

'And I want us to do a hypnobirthing course.'

'Ay? What the flip is hypnobirthing?'

'You'll like it. It's about visualisation. Breathing. And releasing a woman's natural force. We're doing it.'

I switch the laptop back on.

Conversations with a Teenager

'You said you were gonna clean the bathroom at the weekend.'

The Teenager looks through me.

'I will,' she says.

'Last weekend,' I point out.

'I will.'

'You will what?'

'I'll clean the bathroom.'

'You were supposed to clean it last weekend. As in, the previous one.'

'I don't know what day it is.'

'You don't know what day it... a... you know what, I believe you.'

'About what?'

'That you don't know what day it is.'

'I do.'

'You just said... you win.'

'What?'

'I'll clean the bathroom myself. It's like trying to interview David Blaine for a job.'

'Who's David Blaine?'

'A famous street magician from the 90s.'

'I wasn't born then.'

'So?'

'So what?'

'For fu.. sa.. why does that mean you don't know him? You know who Jesus is?'

'Yeah.'

'And he's pretty famous, yeah?'

'Were you alive when Jesus was doing his thing?'

'No.'

'But you know who he is?'

'Yeah, but why does David Blaine want to clean our bathroom?'

'I'm going to bed.'

The Bribery Trap

Fatherhood has changed me. No doubt about it. I'm like a proper grownup. I think differently. I make sensible, well-thought-out decisions. I've become more empathic. Compassionate – I feeeel more. I've discovered if I share my thoughts with The Wife she won't laugh in my face and call me a wuss. In fact, most of the time I find our concerns are aligned. Which is reassuring. I dare to go a little further and suggest that most of the other parents I meet in the world also share many of our worries or feelings of inadequacy. It's comforting to look around the carnage of a soft play area and know we are all just doing the best we can.

Yes, fatherhood has pushed me to grow whilst depleting me of the last dregs of youth from my face. The wrinkles are juicy and numerous around my eyes. I have the thickest grey hairs imaginable poking out of my nose and bunching together inside my ear canals. My mind is often foggy and the days blur. I dig deep to find the energy to play Zombie-Ninjas one more time before bed but miraculously, I don't need to dig very deep to stay up drinking red wine and eating endless packets of crisps once the little bundles of chubbiness have gone to sleep.

I've had periods of being a stay-at-home dad and this has taught me some vital lessons. Always have wipes, food, a book or toy, and a change of clothes in the bag. Basic stuff that comes in handy when faced with an unexpected dog-shit-disaster or an overly long wait in a queue. Actively listen to little ones; talk to them in a way in which you'd like to be spoken to. Don't match their shouts with yours and it helps to get down to their physical level when offering comfort or delivering bad news, such as, "It's time to leave soft play."

It's better to become an expert negotiator and not resort to bribery, said no parent ever! I never realised how intertwined bribery was with parenting but I know now. Oh, how I know now. I kid myself it's just bargaining or being fair but that's complete bollocks. It feels good to say it out loud to be honest.

Unless I offer some kind of sweetener it's impossible to get them to leave anywhere or do anything.

"Yes, you can have a second chocolate bar, just as long as we can leave the park now."

"Yes, you can watch another episode of Paw Patrol, just as long as you understand this is the last one."

When Arlo was a toddler, I could make everything sound amazing.

"Come on, Son, leeeeets get dreeessed!"

He'd drop whatever he was doing and come running over to me with a big smile on his face. Getting dressed usually meant we were going somewhere fun. And he was happy to do what I asked.

But he figured something out.

Why should he stop having fun without a fuss when he can get something out of it?

Now, everything's a battle. Made even more difficult since his wild brother joined the crew. And Ove, he's a whole other level. Bribery doesn't work on children who look down on your feeble efforts with disdain. He takes great pleasure in doing the complete opposite of what you ask and that's enough pleasure for him. Stuff ya chocolate.

In a previous life, I would scoff into my single man's red wine in restaurants while parents pleaded with their kids to be quiet; shoving iPhones into their faces so they can devour the meal in peace before the kids decide it's time to go walkabout through doors with *Staff Only* written on them.

"You'll never see me do that," scoff, scoff, scoff.

"You need to put your foot down, mate," scoff, scoff, scoff.

What a fool. What a naïve fool I was. I really miss that guy.

How did I fall into this bribery trap? Sleep deprivation? Probably. Wanting an easy life? Definitely. But it's not an easy life is it? Not in the end. Eventually, I'll have nothing to give, and then what? When they've tasted all the cakes, watched all the DVDs and drunk all the variations of non-concentrated organic juice this world has to offer, what's next?

I have this vision of Arlo walking into the kitchen while I'm slaving over the stove, watching as he grabs one of my German Beers from the fridge and flicks the top off with the spur on *Woody's* boot then taking a long underserved gulp.

'What you doing with my beer, Son?'

'Your beer? Funny. Get on with tea, Old Man.'

I have an idea. Maybe I've been trying to protect him from feelings of disappointment. When he reacts to a decision which infringes upon his happiness, like leaving a fun event or not eating all the grapes in one sitting - I've plastered over his natural response to disappointment with a reward system that only delays his frustration. It hurts me to see him in pain so I offer unrelated solutions to ease the situation.

But this cannot continue. So what can I do? Better time management for starters.

Example:

- We need to be somewhere for 10 am and begin the process of getting ready the night before. Leaves plenty of time for leeway.
- Simpler days – fewer activities. Rather than try and do shopping in the morning, park midmorning, and library after lunch, just focus on one activity without an agenda. This leaves plenty of space for more spontaneous interactions.
- Finally, my boys are going to get frustrated. Tired. Annoyed. But I think that's only a small percentage of the day compared to the rest which is filled with laughter and fun.

Seriously, I'm like a proper grown-up now. Scary.

Conversations
with a Kid

'I think I want to marry a boy and a girl when I'm older.'

'Covering your bases. Good idea, Son.'

'But I'll wait until I'm much older.'

'Sounds sensible.'

'You'll be dead then.'

'Cheers, Son.

Pizza

Fickle. That's putting it mildly. How can they love me but hate cheese and toast? Then the following week love cheese on toast and hate me? It makes no sense! I'm like the reliable go-to food for parents. A sure thing. Yeah, Hawaiian causes some debate but a crispy thin-based Margherita... What's not to like? Only beans on toast, dippy eggs and soldiers or jam butties come even close to me.

I've seen these boys turn their noses up at chips. Chips! What type of kid will say no to chips, then, when asked what they want instead asks for boiled carrots? Not normal!

I blame the parents of course. These modern types just pander to their children's ridiculous demands. Every meal looks like it's been assembled by a stoned teenager experimenting with the colour beige!

The Dad, I give him his due, he's a trier. He gets this glint in his eye. This look of victory when his boys try something new - nothing exotic, just Cottage Pie or something equally as mundane. Then that glint soon turns to tears I tell you. The next time he places that same mundane meal in front of those boys, the EXACT meal, portion size, temperature, every detail catered for and replicated in exactly the same way, only to be met with, 'I don't like it.'

His expression tells a sad story.

Rage. Pain. Defeat. Repeat.

It just makes no edam sense!

No More Babies

'So that's it, no more babies?' The Wife says.

I hold her hand and look lovingly into her eyes.

'I'd prefer to put my balls in a blender then go through this again.'

'Don't say that! Arlo's amazing.'

'He is. But could we really survive having another baby that sleeps as little as him? I don't even want to think about it.'

She's gutted. I know she's stuck between wanting me to say, "Yeah, let's do it, Babe. Let's see how much sleep deprivation two humans can endure. Let's think of it as a science project.' And "No, piss off."

Piss-off seems much easier than the other option right now.

'Right, well you'd better go and get the snip then cos I'm not going back on the pill.'

'Whoa, calm down. Don't you think that's a bit drastic?'

'Why's it always got to be on the woman?'

Of course, I have a minor responsibility in all of this.

'How about the withdrawal method,' I offer. Jokingly.

She ain't laughing. Got to turn this around quickly.

'Aren't there some natural ways? I'm sure I read something about monitoring temperature. Plus you haven't had a period for ages now. The way that boy keeps draining your boobs we'll be right for a while yet.'

'Not really a long-term option is it?'

'No. I guess not. We could get some condoms from the family planning place. Ribbed for your pleasure.'

She looks at me like I'm the biggest idiot she's ever met in her life, with a *how did I ever let you impregnate me?* kind of expression. I need to take this seriously.

'Babe, are you sad because you won't get to have a little baby again? Is that what it is?'

I've knocked the nail right on the head and The Wife's eyes fill with tears.

'Listen, why don't we get some condoms for a bit? Mix it up with a spot of mutual masturbation and see how we feel in a year or so. You never know, Arlo might be sleeping through by then and we'll be in the right mental state to talk about it properly.'

She wipes her snotty nose.

'So it's not completely off the table?'

'Nothing's ever completely off the table, Babe.'

Balls in a blender! I totally mean it.

'Come here.'

We have a nice long hug, which turns into a nice slow kiss, then right on cue, our beautiful little passion killer wakes up screaming from an afternoon nap in his bedroom and we both go and see him.

'Little boy, Mummy's here, it's okay.'

He calms down and attaches himself to his favourite thing in the world, The Wife's boob.

'We need a night out. I'm gonna ask my mum to come and have him for an evening.'

'But she won't be able to put him to bed.'

'If we don't let her give it a go we'll never know will we? Let's ask her to come early in the evening, we'll go for a meal, smash a bottle of red, eat, smoke a cig then come home to deal with it. What do you reckon?'

I watch her mind complete a full risk assessment.

'Sounds great, let's do it.'

'Yes!'

The following week - I think, could have been a year, another life, the next day, sleep deprivation is no joke - Granny arrives to look after Becca (The Teenager) and Arlo for a few hours.

'Cheers, Mum. We'll be back for 7ish.'

'Don't worry, we'll be fine,' Granny says.

I know The Wife wants to explain in great detail what we have already written down on a piece of paper and given to Granny, but I pull her by the arm towards the gate. This is the first time we've both been separated from Arlo since his birth nearly two years ago.

And he is not happy about it! But we need this!

'He'll be fine when you've gone, don't worry, just go,' Granny says confidently.

The Wife's body is like a rock. All of her motherly instincts are screaming, "He needs me, he needs me," and I'm sure Arlo feels the same but we need this more. We deserve this.

'Come on, Babe."

My voice breaks the spell and she's guided down the path away from the house. It's horrible. Is it supposed to be this hard? The Wife's crying. I'm thirsty. We can still hear Arlo screaming. Then suddenly, it stops. The door has been shut and I make sure The Wife moves in the direction of the Italian restaurant where we have a reservation for an early bird deal.

Five minutes later...

'Shall I call to see if he's okay?'

'No.'

Twelve minutes later...

'I'm just gonna call to see-'

'No.'

Fifteen minutes later at the restaurant ordering wine and food...

'Do you think he's alright?'

'Probably.'

'Why probably?'

'Because I don't know. I can guarantee he's not been left to play with the knives.'

'Why would you say that?'

'Because I trust my mum to take care of him.'

'I'm calling.'

29

'NO.'

Twenty-three minutes later...

'This wine is nice.'

'My boobs are leaking.'

Twenty-five minutes later...

'I just called your mum when I was in the toilet sorting my boob out. He's fine. They're watching *Lion King*.'

'See. Now you can chill out a bit.'

Forty Minutes Later...

My phone rings.

'Is that your mum? Is he okay?'

'I'm just trying to get it out of my pocket.'

'I knew it. Get the bill.'

She stands up.

'It's Becca. Sit down, Babe.'

She reluctantly perches back on the edge of her seat.

'Hi, what's up?'

The Wife is burning a hole through my head with heat vision eyes!

'In the top drawer in our bedroom. Yes. We're having a nice time. We'll see you in an hour or so.'

I turn the phone off and place it on the table.

'Spare dummy.'

She lets out a sigh of relief so heavy, heads turn and glasses rattle on their tables.

We made it through the rest of the evening without interruption. The Wife's trying to act cool like she's not removing my arm from the socket as she pulls me up the street towards our house. I hope that noise I can hear is something other than her grinding her teeth otherwise they're going to be chalk dust by the time we get in.

'Are you okay, Babe?'

'Mm mm.'

Her expression softens and the grinding ends as we arrive at the front door. No screaming baby. The house isn't a pile of burning rubble after all. Nor has a pack of baby-eating wolves escaped from the zoo and figured out where we keep the spare key. I smile and touch her face gently.

'We made it. Our first night together. You look so beautiful.'

'Key.'

'Ay?'

'Get the keys out of your pocket and open the door.'

'Oh yeah.'

The hallway light sparks to life and Becca opens the front door.

'Hi,' Becca says.

'Hey. It's very quiet in there,' The Wife says.

'He's in bed,' Granny says from the shadows of the kitchen.

'No way,' we both say simultaneously.

'I told you he'd be fine.'

Granny steps into the light. She's aged ten years. Plus, I never noticed she had a twitch before. I can already see the gin and tonic she'll be leathering when she gets home.

'You did. I don't know why I was so worried, thanks,' The Wife says.

'Anytime,' Granny says. 'Just not for the next couple of weeks because we're going to Portugal.'

Pretty sure she booked that holiday this evening using her phone.

'That sounds lovely. Thanks again,' The Wife says as she barges past Becca and Granny, then disappears up the stairs.

I turn to give my mum a kiss but she's already running at full speed up the path. Her coat's flailing behind her like Batman's cape and the last thing I see is the soles of her shoes as she dives head-first over the seven-foot bush at the front of the garden.

'See you, Mum.'

I close the door and turn to Becca.

'How was it?' I ask.

'I don't think we'll be seeing her for a while.'

'At least we had tonight. You okay?'

'I'm going to bed. You might not see me for a while either.'

'Haha. Good night.'

After tidying up a little, I open a bottle of red and pour two glasses. The Wife appears wearing a silky dressing gown.

'He's flat out,' she says.

'Amazing. Now if we could just figure out why he won't do that for us, that'd be fantastic.'

She comes over to me and starts touching my ear.

'What you doing? Why are you wearing that dressing gown? It's like eight O'Clock.'

'Thought we'd go upstairs for a bit of, you know?'

'I've just opened the wine.'

She leans forward and gives me a nice kiss – extra tongue.

'Wine's for losers,' I say as I'm led away from the kitchen upstairs.

Less than ten minutes later...

We both stare up at the ceiling. The lovemaking sweat has already been replaced with a cold panicky one. We both feel it. We look into each other's eyes. Somehow we just know that was baby-making sex! Only a single word can describe this feeling.

Shit.

Conversations
with The Wife

I know what she wants.

She thinks she's so clever.

But she's not. Not even a little bit.

'You haven't worn that jumper for ages, it looks great,' she says.

I throw her a half-smile from my end of the sofa.

'Fanks.'

I return to *Outlander*, which she knows I've been waiting to read for ages; just needed to be in the right mood and have no kids doing my head in. And I'm in the right mood!

'You look goood.'

That was embarrassing.

I nod my head.

Turn a page.

'I didn't know you'd been working out.'

Does she really believe I'm that gullible?

'I haven't.'

'Seriously? Wow. Your arms look huge.'

'I don't want huge arms.'

I remain focused on the book in my hand. I can tell that just threw her off. Big time.

'Erm... not huge exactly. Shapely.'

Ha ha. Nice try. Now piss off.

'Hmm mm.' I reply

I push myself a little further into the sofa, clearly showing my intention to stay right here in this spot, reading my book, chilling out, and living these precious childless moments in peace.

Shit. Oh no. She's good. Flipping good! In one silky movement she's raised her feet off the floor, and tucked them under my bum slightly, creating the illusion of needing warmth and comfort when in reality, it's to give me a not-so-gentle shove in the direction of the kitchen.

Sometimes I forget who I'm dealing with. The manipulation. The planning.

'My feet are freezing but you're so waaaaarrrrm,' she says.

There must be a way to fight back!

'Put the heating on if you like?' I offer.

She was not expecting that.

'What? During the day?' She's shocked.

'Yeah, why not. Go for it.'

Having the heating on during the day is a rare occasion. You literally need to have snot icicles hanging from your blue nose before it's turned on. And here I am offering it up on a plate. I glance over at her. She's torn. She can't just ask me to get up and turn it on. No, no, that would spoil the game. It must appear to be of my own

38

choosing, you see. That's the game. On the other hand, she could just get up and sort it herself... but she won't.

'Why? Do you want to turn it on?' she asks.

Do you see what she did there?

'I'm fine. I have my muscley jumper on.'

'I don't want to put the heating on... just for me,' she practically purrs.

Bloody evil genius.

Two can play that game, Bobby Brown!

My eyes remain fixed on *Outlander* as I reach behind the sofa, like any thoughtful husband would, and grab her a blanket.

'There you go, Bobby.'

'Ay?'

'Nothing.'

'Okay. Thanks.'

A minute later...

Her feet are now making me really uncomfortable. Her toenails are practically slicing my spinal cord as she wriggles her feet against my lower back under the guise of generating warmth.

I smile at her.

She smiles back.

Wriggle, wriggle, slice, slice. Go on, slice away, I hope you sever it! You'll have to get a new slave then and I'll be able to read my book in peace. Just hurry up about it, cos you're doing my head in! I reckon her toes must be aching by now. She's willing to sacrifice her own comfort just to force me off the sofa and into the kitchen, but I won't give in. Not today.

'So comfy,' she lies.

'Hmm mm.'

'Did you buy any biscuits yesterday?'

She's already scoffed half the packet.

'Hmm mm.'

'Which ones.'

'Rich Tea.'

'Perfect to dunk in a brew.'

THERE! SHE FINALLY SAYS THE WORD BREW OUT
LOUD! THE FAÇADE IS OVER!

'If you say so.'

Now she's smacking her lips together and rubbing her throat to
indicate how dry it is.

'Cough, cough.'

She's piling it on.

We're entering the endgame now.

'Are you thirsty, Babe?' I ask.

'Yeah, I'd love a bre -'

'Here.'

I look into her eyes. Her lovely face. I smile and slowly reach towards the side of the sofa; her eyes follow the movement of my hand. She knows what's coming and I know she knows and it feels soooo good. So Righteous.

'Here you go.'

I pass her a bottle of water.

Haha. Not today, Wife!

'Fanks,' she says.

Victory. Nowhere left to go. Game – set – match. Now piss off and leave me be.

'Is that your phone ringing?'

Shit. It's in the kitchen.

'It's fine.'

'It could be important.'

'I don't get important calls.'

'It could be school or nursery?'

'It won't be.'

'You don't know that.'

'I do.'

'Answer the phone.'

'No.'

'Why you being weird?'

'I'm not.'

'You are.'

'I just want to read *Outlander* in peace.'

'You can. Just answer the phone first.'

'Right.'

Her aching toes give it one last hurrah and kindly help me up off the sofa. She's flipping beaming. Radiant. I turn away so she can't see that every fibre of my being is oozing with disappointment and defeat. My face cannot lie. I arrive at the kitchen just as the phone stops ringing.

'Who was it?'

'Shitty private number.'

'That's annoying.'

Three, two, one...

'Stick the kettle on, Babe.'

They're Coming

I look around the quiet bedroom.

It's morning but there are no kids jumping on my head.

What the flip is going on? This never happens.

The Wife is still sleeping. She looks peaceful.

It's light outside. Birds are singing.

Hang on... when did my hair grow back?

The Wife, who is Rachel from *Friends* grabs my wrist.

45

'Do you like your new hair?' Rachel asks.

I nod and smile.

Her grip tightens.

'They're coming,' she hisses.

I open my eyes. It's cold. Dark. Neither day or night.

Two loud thuds from the other bedroom disturb the silence.

I turn to The Wife. She's staring blankly up at the ceiling.

She pulls the cover tight to her chin.

'They're coming,' she whispers.

Tricky World Of Parenting

I'm turning into a massive softy. And I don't mean my midriff which already resembles a pack of jam swiss rolls. I'm talking about my inner workings – those things I've avoided since childhood. You know what I mean? My emo... ahem. Those fee... ahem. You know, don't make me say it! Okay. Here we go. I'm becoming more in-tune with my emotions. I have deeper feelings about my life and family. There, I said it. Life used to be so simple. Now there's all this extra stuff to think about. It's very unsettling.

Did I ever imagine parenting would have this effect on me? Not at all. Was I naïve? Absolutely! Do I blame the kids for making me look inside and consider the notion of personal growth? A resounding yes!

It's my own fault really. I could have been one of those full-time working dads who get an hour or two in the evening and then cram it all into the weekend. Not me. I wanted to be present. I wanted to be there during these early years because The Wife assured me it was the most important time in a child's development. In our relationship.

When I was a kid, no one ever used phrases like development. You were dragged up and on Fridays, you got a Twix and a can of pop. On super special occasions, you got a chippy tea and you were bloody grateful for it. Especially if you got a white barm cake as well (some of you might not know what a barm cake is and that's okay.)

Now there are all these phrases and buzzwords which make it difficult to navigate this tricky world of parenting. The possibility of feeling guilty is there at every turn. I wasn't even fully aware of what guilt felt like before becoming a parent. Blissful ignorance was a preferred state of being. Not anymore. Now I know. And so I've learnt, with regret, that when you feel that guilt, stuffing your kids with chocolate, a chippy tea, buying them toys or any type of material grand gesture isn't the way to solve the issue.

Who knew?

I spend a lot of time with my boys. The Wife is career orientated whereas I'm more domesticated. I love nothing more than noticing the right kind of light breeze, combined with just enough sunshine, then getting the washing on the line. Makes my day. I appear to be the only human in our house capable of picking clothes up off the floor or emptying the recycling. And if I didn't prepare the meals, they'd all have scurvy by now.

There's not much time for anything else. Having a parent stay home brings financial hardship. One income isn't enough to thrive exactly. But as someone who has been in and out of adult education, I've learnt to stretch the shopping money further by making tough choices. Two-ply toilet paper is just enough, as long as your fingers don't go through that is. Bit of trial and error with that one. Home-baking, batch cooking, boxes of wine, stuff like that.

Budgeting is a skill.

Being at home has boosted my tolerance levels because there's a definite tendency to want to scream more than normal when you're with your kids, day in, day out. I get it, they're my kids. It's my responsibility to care for them, who else would do that better? But it's not like I have extensive parenting knowledge. One day I was a solitary beast then the next I'm part of a pack. A very strange pack.

No one at work has ever wiped their shit on my trousers while I wasn't looking or screamed in my face for cutting a sandwich at the wrong angle.

I've had to evolve. Or medicate!

And by doing so a pattern has begun to emerge. One I'm grateful for.

Parenting is a constant cycle of reacting – reflecting – unlearning.

Let me explain.

Say you react to something in the way you were shown as a child; your child does something wrong like hit their sibling and take their toy away. You react by snatching it back and shouting. After you've shouted and made the situation worse, it's time, if you're able, to reflect on whether that was the best course of action and how it might have concluded with a more peaceful approach.
Once reflected upon it's then possible to unlearn that reaction so you're equipped with a better strategy for next time.

It's taken me a long time to come to this realisation and I absolutely still get it wrong. And that's okay. I'm constantly looking for new ways to learn about my boys and how I can better understand their needs. I often sit and watch them play, with as little interference as possible, even if it gets heated. I literally sit, observe, and feel closer to them, sometimes gaining a greater understanding of their personalities.

In the space of fifteen minutes, they live through so many emotions. It must be exhausting for them. It's exhausting for me! It's a wonder I don't take a nap during the day myself.

Taking a hands-on approach to parenting has brought up so much stuff from my childhood which I'd simply concluded as being just the way it goes. When in fact, trauma can disguise itself in many forms. Addiction and anger are just two lovely little issues I've battled with for as long as I can remember.

Picking at all these scabs from the past is not what I signed up for when I became a parent, but I wouldn't change it. It's made me a better person. More forgiving of myself and others. Even if I've decided to end certain relationships because of the knowledge I've acquired, it doesn't mean I haven't forgiven them. It just means I've developed a new set of ground rules for myself and my family which no longer includes negative or dysfunctional relationships.
React – reflect – unlearn.

It's not a bad mantra for life in general and you're free to steal it. It's possibly the only parenting tip I've got to offer. The rest is usually more like; try not to scream at your kids in public because it makes

51

it look like you do it all the time. And if possible, it's probably better not to drink booze before 11 am.

But if you need to, *Bucks Fix* is probably best.

Pretend it's Christmas.

Going Mainstream

I had a vision of the dad I was going to be. It involved being zen-like in my approach to behaviour management; no need for raised voices. I would intuitively decipher my child's emotions – bring about calming resolutions with empathy and patience. Gentle parenting.

I was going to be the gentlest parent ever!

Gentle but fair. Approachable. Open to negotiation. Bedtimes were going to be magical. I was going to tuck my little one into bed after story time, kiss his clammy forehead, switch on the night light and leave him to fall asleep independently. He'd be secure in the knowledge that mum and dad were downstairs drinking herbal tea and listening to *The Chimp Paradox* on Audible. Understanding ourselves was going to help us understand the needs of our children.

Ha! Nonsense.

That vision was obliterated very early on. Along with many other things like going gluten-free, not using technology as a third parent, veganism, bribery, and the list goes on. Even though so many things have changed, been removed, shifted around or sneakily brought back into play, there was one thing I didn't foresee changing; our plan to home-educate was set in stone.

It was immoveable.

We had designed so much of our life around this idea that we never stopped to consider it wouldn't happen.

The plan was simple. After nursery, Arlo would attend a Forest School once or twice a week. We'd find some clubs: Performing arts, swimming, whatever he wanted. Because being cool, child-led parents we were going to be democratic in our approach to education. He would have time at home with us to learn about important things like cleaning the fridge, washing clothes, ironing clothes, making beds, and cooking tea. The list was endless.

This boy was going to be ready to move out by the age of 10!

As it turned out, Arlo really wanted to go to school. Really wanted to go. We wouldn't be cool, child-led parents if we didn't listen to him, would we? We live around the corner from a primary school and each day Arlo watched the children walking in their uniform towards it and he wouldn't stop asking about it.

'Where are those children going?'

'School, Son.'

'I want to go.'

'Really?'

'Yeah.'

'You have to go five days a week.'

'I don't mind.'

'You have to do as you're told.'

That got him thinking.

'You have to sit behind a desk most of the day and listen to the teacher.'

'Not all day though?'

'No, not all day.'

'Do you get to play with your friends sometimes?'

'You do.'

'I love playing with my friends.'

The home-schooling community offers a wide range of opportunities to meet up and socialise with other children. You get discounts for events and attractions within term time. Plus, several other perks and you aren't restricted by inflated holiday prices which is a massive bonus.

But Arlo had a few negative experiences with some older children and, although they were isolated incidents, it left us feeling slightly put off by the idea of home-ed.

In the end, we attended two open days at different primary schools, and he didn't want to leave either one. He loved the smart uniforms. Classrooms packed with children. Young energetic teachers filled with hope wearing freshly ironed, stainless clothes. All smiling and happy.

Maybe they were faking it?

We couldn't tell. Either way, Arlo saw this world and wanted to be part of it. We couldn't ignore this. It was a curveball we did not expect.

So he started at school. I didn't want him to go. I'll admit it was for selfish reasons. I was going to miss him. He's just so little. In

Scandinavian schools, the children don't start until the age of seven. I would prefer that. Arlo's just a baby at barely four years old. He's super vulnerable; brimming with an infectious enthusiasm for life which can sometimes cause communication problems with other children.

Sometimes with adults too.

They don't know how to handle him. I was scared that he'd be bullied if I'm honest. I wanted to protect him for as long as possible.

But I'm also a realist.

I can't be there for him forever. But mainstream school kind of feels like the final nail in the coffin of our alternative lifestyle choices. What's next? Am I going to start eating white bread again? Shiny ham? Watching football again? Maybe I'll just get a mundane nine-to-five in a boring office where I can eat my white bread, shiny ham butties and talk about last night's game!

Okay, there are some positives. There is this writing malarkey I dip in and out of which I've been able to pursue with a little more enthusiasm. Ove gets more of my attention. I'm batch cooking like a pro. The house is looking reasonably clean, and the ironing bag only weighs about half a tonne now which is a vast improvement.

I found a shirt the other day I had completely forgotten I still owned. I was like, no way, I look amazing in this shirt! The garden and mud kitchen look organised, and the car no longer resembles the bottom of a skip. Things are looking good. But do I actually care about those things? Not really. I'd much prefer to have Arlo at home with me. I'm selfish like that.

Conversations
with a Kid

'How old are you, Dad?'

'40.'

'That's really old.'

'Er, it's not that old actually.'

'You're going to die soon.'

'Cheers, Son.'

Eighth Wonder
of the World

I knew something was off that day. We had plans in place but the weather had other ideas. Plus for some reason, my boys decided they were going to say no to everything I offered as a solution whether that was alternative destinations or food choices.

'Do you want slightly toasted bread with a fine layer of butter and a generous dollop of sticky jam spread evenly on top my little ones?' I asked.

What they heard...

'I hate you.'

'Why don't we paint pictures of monsters, stick them up all over the house then walk around shooting at them with those dart gun things your mum hates?'

What they heard...

'No, you can't watch the telly or play on any electrical device today.'

I was getting desperate. A meltdown was imminent. Everything was everywhere and the house was feeling very cramped. So I said it. The words I always regret uttering.

'Do you want to go soft-play?'

That got their attention. Then I suddenly remembered soft-play is a fucking nightmare. It's a sure way to ensure both my boys will have the shits by tomorrow. All those kids running around like wild beasts with sticky warm hands covered in hidden germs from bum cracks, genitals, and that bit of the toilet rim no adult touches without rubber gloves!

Kids are disgusting.

But that day I witnessed something so unbelievable it's difficult to describe. When we arrived at soft-play I could hear the pandemonium inside the building. If you don't know what pandemonium means look it up. It definitely doesn't mean serene calming tones.

Arlo was off the second we arrived in the place, throwing his shoes in the air behind him like he was running towards the sea. I caught one before it dislodged a piece of cake from a hungry mum's shaking hands and the other just because it looked cool and basically headed straight towards me. I turned back to Arlo but only saw the back of his head and another boy as they disappeared into the abyss of the soft-play equipment.

Ove stayed with me. He was going in the carrier for at least half an hour for a sleep whether he wanted to or not. But there was something about that boy Arlo was with. An ancient, reptilian part of my brain was alerted. Something disgusting was present and I just knew Arlo needed me.

I picked Ove up and slipped him into the carrier. Together we approached the mouth of the large climbing, slidey, dirty ball pit area where only the brave will enter. Ove looked at me with his pure blue knowing eyes.

'Yes, Son. We must go in.'

He pointed towards the flashy arcade game in the corner and mumbled.

'No. Arlo needs us.'

I tightened the carrier strap - I wasn't going to lose this one, and we entered the darkness. Strange calling cries sounded from several directions. The air was damp with farts and pissy pants.

Lightweight punch bags hung from metal bars and dangled in front of us. We pushed through. There was no going back.

A long-haired dungaree-wearing toddler was in the corner headbutting the spongy wall and singing about fruits and vegetables that keep you alive. I went against my better judgement and asked him if he needed help. He stopped. Slowly turned his head without moving his body and began laughing hysterically.

We left him to it as he turned away and continued.

Arlo and the boy ran across a rickety bridge above us. Pieces of ancient fluff fell down around us. I only glimpsed the bottom of their socks but I knew it was them. We took a left and began climbing up a strappy stairwell to the next level where the lost children from *Mad Max* were wandering around in small packs.

They'd been long forgotten by their carers, parents, or whoever it was who'd brought them to this barren land. I took a deep breath and held Ove's head against my chest as we walked slowly towards the exit on the other side of the space. I hoped to achieve this without getting noticed.

But it was hopeless.

'Dadda?' asked a child wearing a potato sack for a dress.

I didn't make eye contact and stepped slowly to the side into the shadows. She wandered towards an inflated tube with a clown face.

'Dadda?' she repeated.

I placed my back against the padded wall and quickly realised we were not alone.

'Daddy?' a boy with half a haircut asked.

I shook my head and shushed him, but it was too late. The docile pack had been awakened. They'd never seen a man under sixty years old on a workday and they wanted one. Badly. Kids dropped from the padded scaffold all around us. Others dragged themselves over brightly coloured patched-up barriers. Their eyes were wild with expectation.

Ove squeezed my shoulder.

'I know, Son. I love you.'

We continued to move slowly against the padded wall towards the exit. An opening I hadn't noticed appeared and a well-used *Woody* impersonator stepped forward.

'Daddy?'

'Look, there's Buzz.'

He turned away.

But we had caused too much attention and the children had organised. They just stood silently. Staring. A gap opened up in the pack and a haggard-looking Snow White walked towards us. Smaller children hissed at her. She let some of them smell her hands and touch her dress but she scolded others away with a sharp look. They recoiled into the shadows screeching and howling in emotional torment.

Snow White stopped a metre away and looked at Ove in the carrier.

'My Daddy,' she said.

The pack slapped the floor and stamped their feet as they shuffled towards us.

We were done for.

Suddenly, from out of the darkness to our left, flickers of light began to sting the children's eyes as dangly strips of fabric were disturbed by a chubby fist. I took the opportunity and slipped away towards the exit.

All eyes turned towards a little toddler wobbling his way into the centre of the pack.

He looked around. Innocent. No sense of danger. He held out a hand which clutched a white semi-chewed ball of deconstructed toast.

'Toast?' he exclaimed.

The pack completely forgot about my existence and headed straight for that poor boy. He looked confused at first, then angry, as the pack began clawing at the prize in his grip. This gave me the vital seconds required to scramble to safety onto a platform at the mouth of the exit.

I looked over my shoulder one last time as a *Peppa Pig* and *Paw Patrol* enthusiast wrestled him to the floor.

'Thank you,' I whispered. 'Your sacrifice will not be in vain.'

He never stood a chance.

The higher we climbed the hotter it got. Greece in the height of summer hot. I thought somebody was cooking kebabs in the ball pit but it was the smell from my armpits which were oozing toxins stored from Creamfields Festival 1999.

Some fresh-faced older kids appeared waving small balls in the air and shouting in a dialect I couldn't understand. I dodged, nudged and pushed past them and continued to climb to the top.

It became silent. Darkened. A chill filled the air and the damp patches under my arms and across my chest froze instantly. Ove sensed the change in temperature and began to squirm.

'We're here,' I told him.

He stopped. I nodded. We scrambled onto the final platform where Arlo and his friend were sitting on the floor passing a dented ball back and forth between them. Arlo looked up.

'Hi, Dad,' he shouted.

His new friend turned suddenly before I could reply. Ove grasped my hand. The luminous snot hanging from this kid's nose was nothing short of miraculous. I was hypnotised by its sheer otherworldliness. I wanted to prod it with a stick but I had no stick. No sense of space or time. Was it real? Is anything real?

This living organism attached to that child's face made me question my very existence.

I acted swiftly.

'You need to go find your mum, or whoever you're with, sharpish and ask them to wipe your nose, mate.'

He knew. His eyes told me so. I respected him at that moment. He had the presence of mind to not wipe it on his thin sleeve - he would've needed an arm longer than an orangutan to achieve this anyway and instead, chose to continue living his best life. Allowing this eighth wonder of the world to exist on his face. Neither boy was alarmed by this new organ growing on his philtrum.

But unlike these children, I have a keen eye for such things, so I pointed with a finger and nudged him with a toe towards the slide.

'Go on – go, get, go on.'

He rolled away and slid down the slide headfirst on his back, not breaking eye contact with me for a moment. Neither did it. I tried to overt my eyes but it was simply too amazing. He disappeared from view. I removed Ove from the carrier and we both hugged Arlo, who had no idea he'd been in the presence of a medical marvel.

We explored a rope swing for a while then destroyed my knees chasing them along half a mile of solid plastic tunnelling before arriving at the final bumpy multiple-lane slide.

'Shall we go down, boys? Get a snack?'

'Yeah,' they shouted.

We took up our positions. I turned to my right.

'Are you ready, Arlo?'

He was. I turned to the left.

'Ove?'

He was ready too.

I turned back to Arlo and his friend had returned with a handful of chocolate buttons melting in his grasp. Chocolate was smeared all over his now snot-less face.

'Chocolate,' he announced.

Over his shoulder, Snow White approached with her gang following close behind - licking their lips. Nostrils flared. They could smell the chocolate buttons. The chubby toddler who had fed them the bread was one of them now except he looked thinner and broken.

There wasn't a second to lose. My boys would be next!

'Look, more friends,' I said.

I pointed towards the pack and pushed both my boys down the slide to safety.

We never looked back.

Bonding without Boobs

While preparing for the birth of Arlo, The Wife and I thought we had it covered. From hypnobirthing and home birth to half-inflated birth pools, it was all under control. After the birth, The Wife was going to make cakes, drink sparkling wine and sleep for eight hours a night while our calm bundle of joy slept right through.

Ah, to dream!

One minor issue we forgot to discuss, was . . . me. What was my job once he arrived? We planned the pregnancy and the birth. The Wife was going to be his meal ticket, but we never discussed what it would be like for me. What type of dad was I going to be? What was my role?

It was so clear leading up to the birth. Feed the wife, scratch her back, and say nice things. Assist with difficult jobs like putting socks on and making cheese on toast, in that special way only I seem to know how. I also had a defined role during the birth. The knowledge gained during hypnobirthing training gave me responsibility. I was able to whisper words and phrases of encouragement into The Wife's ear that reminded her how amazing she was doing and that everything was alright.

Watching The Wife transform into a warrior moving from bed to floor, to on top of the wardrobe and back again was something I'll never forget. Eventually, she found her way into the birthing pool and I have no idea how much time passed but at some point, Arlo's head was visible under the water.

I kind of looked around the room at the midwife and asked with my eyes whether it was normal to have your head underwater for this long. She didn't appear bothered so I just went along with it. Moments later a little purple, slimy torpedo popped into the water.

Passing Arlo into The Wife's arms was a life-changing experience and the relief, after all the appointments and pregnancy chat leading up to that moment, was huge. It went better than I'd expected but in the same breath, it was still super intense and scary.

Once the medical bits and bobs were sorted, The Wife relaxed skin-to-skin with Arlo and after a while, it was my turn. Finally, I was able to experience the first snippets of physical entanglement with my son. Amazing. Beautiful. Later, close to sunrise, I was knackered and suddenly had an unexpected thought; *what do I do now?*

He was too small to play Poker and too young to drink wine. *What do I do now?* What a silly thought. I brushed it away and we all slept for a while. I woke three hours later feeling refreshed and excited about the day ahead. Becca emerged from her pit and got in on the skin-to-skin action too.

The three of them shared some time together while my man duties began. Clean the room, empty the pool, and cook nice food. Crack open a bottle of sparkly and greet the few guests who came and went. It was a relaxed couple of days. Then things started to get a bit stressful. Arlo was struggling to latch onto The Wife's boob and she was becoming engorged. Engorged is the kind of word I wish remained a mystery to me!

She was in pain. He was distressed. I felt completely useless.

Eventually, when we were contemplating buying formula, it happened. He fed and that boy has hardly been off the boob since!

However, doubt reared its ugly head again.

How do I emulate a feeling that comes so naturally to her?

How do I bond without boobs?

I suddenly felt like an intruder and I can't sensibly explain why. I changed his nappies and tried to comfort him the best I could, but he only seemed happy with a boob in his mouth.

It's one of those overlooked issues, I think. A bottle-fed baby gets passed around like a spliff at a party, everyone gets a go, before it's returned to the person who made it. Breastfed babies are like those spoiled kids who make you sit and wait on the floor while they have extra turns on their Sega Mega Drive because "It's my game!" Spoilt! You know who you are.

In my head, not being able to feed him seemed to take a bonding opportunity away from me. Was I being selfish? Immature? Jealous maybe? The problem was I wasn't educated in the ways of breastfeeding. I'd never known anyone who breastfed or considered that it would affect our lives so significantly. And it did.

The Wife was finishing her degree that year and when Arlo was six months old, he was with me for roughly four hours a day, three to four times a week. The Wife expressed, which wasn't fun for her, but it provided Arlo with just enough liquid nectar until she came home.

So there I was, giving him a bottle of expressed milk like I'd wanted to and I realised, it wasn't comforting to him, it was just fuel. Once he was finished, he'd discard the bottle like it was a rotten banana

74

skin. I couldn't use the bottle in the same way The Wife used the boobs. It wasn't the same. I had to find my own way.

This is where sling-wearing really worked for me. And, being the master of distraction, I found myself doing a variety of things to connect with him. Funny faces and fart noises, no problem. But what calmed him the most, was singing. I was self-conscious at first, and rightly so, I'd never sung out loud as an adult unless intoxicated and reading the words off a screen, but I worked through it.

I made up silly songs about poo, flowers, the weather, and willies. You name it, I've got a lyric. I can sing *Five Little Ducks* in a variety of accents now. I even added a new verse with monkeys.

As he crawled I could chase him from room to room, over and over and over again until my shredded knees could take no more. Mama might have milky boobs but she doesn't have kneecaps made of steel! Now he's a toddler weighing around 20st of pure chub, I get a free workout while throwing him in the air and dancing around the kitchen to Rage Against the Machine (a band he likes for reasons unexplained) while making tea.

We have certain games we play outside and around the house that are just for us. I know his expressions. I know when to calm it down and when he needs a snack. I've learnt this and more through trial and error.

He forgives me quickly when I make a mistake the same way I forgive him when he smashes a book or wooden toy into my face when I least expect it for the millionth time.

He's my son and I'm his dad and one day when he's bigger I'm gonna tell him all about these feelings so that one day if he ever becomes a dad himself, he'll know it's okay to be vulnerable. He can bond without boobs. I might leave out the toy smashing in the face bit though. Don't want to ruin all the surprises.

Bank of Tears

For reasons which are unknown to him, he has never cried from happiness. Shedding a tear about something painful is hard enough so happy crying is very unlikely. There have been many opportunities but the response just doesn't arise inside him. He wants it to. Isn't that a normal response to the emotional experiences parents encounter in their family lives?

Watching his wife walk down the aisle towards him on a perfect day surrounded by close family and friends would have been such an opportunity. But nothing. Supporting his wife while she home birthed his children is another. His sweat merged with hers. She hung from his shoulders. They breathed in nature's magic together. He experienced the great relief of holding both his warrior wife and healthy baby... but still... nothing.

No tears of joy or relief. No tears of anything! He's just not wired that way. He's learnt to accept that about himself. He remembers tears of pain streaming down his young face as a small child - hurt and alone in his room trying to make deals with whatever supernatural force might be passing by. He can see his teenage years so clearly – screaming at the sky and smashing his fists against the walls, unable to understand the unfairness of life. Then his twenties arrived, and his bank of tears had run dry. Instead of shouting, he danced with shiny chemicals inside him and had no time for frustration or sadness.

Over time, as his relationships became more complicated and he shared his life with others, the bank of tears was replenished but the vault was locked and the key lost.

This meant developing strategies to prevent the tear bank from becoming overwhelmed. The vault was fitted with a new combination lock. One that can be opened with a little forward thinking and just the right factors in place to open it. He achieves this by observing his feelings. Taking note. Recognising when the vault needs a release. Then, he acts.

There're a few essential items required to help him open the vault just enough to ease the pressure but not let it run dry again. This is a process designed through trial and error, over several years of experimentation.

Essential Factors:
- Two bottles of red wine. Minimum.
- Rolling tobacco and liquorice papers.
- Quiet, tidy, undisturbed space.
- Access to different genres of film.

The Process:

His wife goes to bed, taking the two boys with her. He tidies up the carnage which has been littered throughout the house. He cleans the kitchen and fills the dishwasher while the red wine breathes. When his jobs are complete, he settles in front of the television, drinks, chooses a suitable film and drinks some more.

Happiness and sadness begin to merge as he watches a selection of films with the right emotional kick. He drinks his wine and has the occasional smoke. Searching for the right combination. It's not always successful.

At least twice a year, he'll find the perfect combination in this drunken state which unlocks the vault for a short time. Not a blubbery type of crying, nothing that would get out of control, just a comfortable flow of tears released.

Afterwards, he'll watch the rest of the film, maybe watch another, finish his wine then go to bed with a warm satisfied feeling inside his belly. And for a period of time, while the vault is slowly filling up again, he'll be just fine. But always watching. Checking on himself. Ready for next time. Hoping that one day he won't need a process or a list of essential factors to unlock the bank of tears.

Nipples with Purpose

I've been staring up at the ceiling for over two hours trying to get Ove to sleep. I know every single inch of it: The strange bit of crusty something that looks a bit like Jesus which the Sunday Sport Newspaper would have paid good money to photograph once, the dead spider in the corner, a lump of jam, I think. I've plotted a route through every bump, swirl, and crack from above the doorway, which I hope to escape through, and the window, which I'm considering jumping headfirst out of. But I can't escape. Ove, the boy who was supposed to sleep is furiously sucking on his diddy and using my nipple as a comforter. Vigorously!

Ha-ha. I asked for this.

I actually asked for this by telling The Wife we needed a change. And what a change we've made. She's downstairs sipping wine, dipping crisps into moist things, laughing her arse off watching YouTube videos while I'm being used and abused. Why couldn't I be one of those inconsiderate dads? I know loads of them, and their lives are amazing! I tell these lucky bastards about some of the ways we co-parent and how we work as a team, this is usually while having the occasional pint when I'm allowed to go out, and most of the time they just stare at me in utter disbelief. It's just not on their radar to lie in bed for over two hours while their kid twiddles, rubs and pinches their nipple until it no longer resembles a nipple.

It's just a scab now. A strange scab that was useless but now has a purpose.

I don't want nipples with purpose!

It's a sacrifice I was willing to make because I didn't think Ove would care about my purposeless nipples. I'd never used them for anything myself. It never occurred to me that he would consider them an adequate substitute for The Wife's lovely boobs. But I was wrong. So terribly, terribly wrong.

But we had to make a change. The Wife had Arlo clawing at her chest for three years and Ove was supposed to be different. Everyone said, "You never get the same kid twice."

Wrong!

She endured three years with Arlo sucking the last dregs of moisture from her body then nearly two years of it happening all over again with the other one. And they don't just lie there suckling calmly. Oh no! These beasts want to twist around, do the crab, to drink upside down while walking up the wall. Still attached! Not once did either one of them just have a refreshing drink from each boob, thank The Wife, and then go about their day redecorating the walls with yoghurt and unidentified stickiness.

It's all or nothing with these boys.

I used to be the one downstairs drinking wine and living my best life. Now I'm stuck here staring at the flipping ceiling dying for a wee but scared to go too soon. He hasn't moved for twelve minutes now. His grip on my scabby nipple has gone limp; always a good sign. His breathing is loud and annoying. Way over the top. Arlo's at the other end of the double mattress completely knocked out snoring equally as loud. We never thought the day would come that he would be classed as the "good" sleeper.

We never believed we'd have a second child with recurring ear infections either. No one deserves that kind of torture. It appears we were wrong. But surviving one sleep thief has equipped us with a few valuable lessons. Don't think just because the little beast hasn't moved for a few minutes that he's sleeping. They like to do this fake breathing thing once they've accepted that the good shapely bit of your nipple has turned to mush, and there's nothing left to twiddle.

Their breathing becomes rhythmic. The room calms. You start thinking about that wine. You allow the sensations in your body to return to normal because your bladder is set to burst.

It's deception!

Why don't I just get up and leave? I'm glad you asked. If I just get up now and head to the door without checking if he's asleep first, and he's lying there all chubby-faced and wide-eyed, this would have been for nothing and I'll be stuck here for another hour, easy. Might as well kiss those crisps and dips goodbye!

So I won't be moving a muscle for at least another five minutes. I'm not even going to turn my head to see if he's looking at me. I'm going to stay right here, watery-eyed and annoyed for another five minutes, at least, then I'll slowly turn my head and check out the situation.

The Wife's laughing again downstairs.

Nothing's that funny.

Go on.

Drink the wine.

Eat the crisps.

Make sure you don't choke!

God, I need a wee.

That's it. Sod it. I'm making a move. I turn my head. I half expect to see Ove's blue eyes shining at me in the darkness but they're not. He's sleeping. No doubt. Now for the tricky manoeuvre - navigating my way off the noisiest mattress ever created.

Gentle roll to my left, straight off the bed, landing on all fours like a cat in one fluid, well-rehearsed, movement.

Silence. Perfectly executed.

Next, the squeaky floorboards between the door and my freedom. The trick here is to stay as close to the wall as possible. The carpet is less worn, and the boards are sturdier. Now in a press-up position, I stretch across the room with my right arm and leg and, in one swift, acrobatic movement, I move across the space and push myself into a standing position with my back flat against the wall.

Then wait.

Five seconds...

Don't breathe.

I look down at my beautiful boys and pray I don't see their faces again until at least 6 am at least. Now, the freedom shuffle. I edge towards the door. The floorboards groan a little, but the soothing classical music covers my tracks. I reach out and push the door and it opens effortlessly, and silently because I drown the hinges with WD40 every flipping night.

Oh, I can taste that wine.

I continue with the freedom shuffle toward the adult world that's calling to me. *Come, drink, smoke, and fiddle with The Wife's earlobe. Come. COME!* One final look over my shoulder, oh shit, oh shit, the baby monitor, the flipping monitor, I've not switched it on.

You idiot! You rookie! Sod it, they'll be fine... but they won't.

I know what must be done.

It must be switched on.

I must go back.

I need to be able to hear the slightest sniff of them waking up. The slightest deviation in their breathing. An out-of-place groan or sniffle, and I'll be up in a shot with a dummy and warm milk so it doesn't turn into an absolute screaming nightmare.

I need it switched on.

I'm going back in.

I make my way back into the darkness, reverse freedom shuffle, but for some cruel joke of the Gods, every floorboard seems to be creaking louder than a theatrical barn door in a storm.

CREAK. Shuffle. CREAK. Shuffle. CREEEEAAAAK.

Oh for fucks sake, why have you forsaken me, cruel Gods?

Wait...

Arlo just kicked Ove in the leg. Ove kicked him back. They're jostling for position. The great top and tail battle has begun. All I can do is watch and hope it doesn't escalate.

As quickly as it began it ends. Both boys flip on their sides and face the wall away from me. I hold my breath. Sweat drips off my nose. My armpits are burning with a toxic stench. This is my moment. I lean down, stretching with a finesse I didn't know my hamstrings would allow, flick the switch on then turn and dive straight out of the room onto the landing, closing the door gently with a touch from an outstretched toe as I fly gracefully through the air landing face first onto the floor.

I don't move - the dust settles - a minute passes.

Nothing. I get up off the floor. My bones are aching. My nipples feel like they've been involved in a nipple-twisting marathon. But I made it. Two and a half hours. I could literally have watched *Lord of the Rings* or flown to Spain in that time, but none of that matters now because I made it! The boys could wake up at any moment, so now, I will commence with drinking two and a half hours' worth of red wine in less than fifteen minutes!

Goodnight fuckers!

Sofa

Why didn't I come with an instruction manual? Everything else does. Not like it would matter with these kids. They just don't know how to use me properly. I'm too good for them really. I was designed for comfort. For relaxing on. I'm not a spaceship. I'm not a bus or a castle for fucks sake!

Excuse the language but I get so stressed. I look like a mess. I'm creased. Saggy in places that used to be tight and firm. I've faded. It's like the colour from my fabric vanished overnight. I used to be so vibrant - healthy looking. I smell weird now. Like pissy-damp-crusty-meat-pie that's been left out in the sun too long.

Would it hurt the parents to get them dressed now and again? Sofas aren't capable of retching but when those boys were learning to wipe their own arses, let me tell you, those were dark days!
But the biggest problem I have, the one thing that really ruins my day is that game *The Floor is Lava*. How I wish they'd never seen that show on Netflix. It's completely ruined my life. I hate being used improperly and I hate shitty arses but I fucking hate *The Floor is Lava*.

Excuse the language.

Conversations
with Myself

Breathing exercises and gratitude journal complete. House is quiet. Peaceful. All is good in the world. Not a single worry to think about. Time for a full eight hours of sleep.

Lights off.

Mind: Do you remember that time when...

Me: In through the nose for six, out of the mouth for eight.

Mind: In for six and out for eight makes no sense.

Me: Can we not do this tonight?

Mind: What?

Me: This shit. Just leave me alone.

Ten seconds...

Me: You're such a dick.

Mind: You said to leave me alone so I did.

Me: I know you though don't I? You would have waited until I was just about to fall asleep then said something stupid like, why didn't they just fly the huge eagles from the final film in Lord of the Rings to the volcano and chuck the ring in at the beginning, and save them from all the pain and death?

Ten seconds...

Mind: That's brilliant. Why didn't they?

Me: I don't know but there must have been a logical reason. I shouldn't have brought it up.

Mind: That's baffled my head. Can't stop thinking about it now.

Me: Now you know how I feel.

Mind: I do. And I'm sorry.

Me: That's okay. Goodnight.

Mind: Night.

Thirty minutes later...

Mind: Do you think it was something to do with the ring's powerful influence over less intelligent creatures or something? Maybe Sauron would have commanded the eagles straight to the gates of Mordor if the ring was in their possession?

Five seconds later...

Me: I'm happy with that conclusion.

Mind: Cool.

Me: Night.

Mind: One more thing.

Me: Go on...

Mind: Why don't we use the Nutribullet anymore?

Me: Please fuck off.

The Toddler and the Telly

We sold our television and it felt amazing! The thought of not having one was a little alternative – even for home-birthing, baby-wearing, co-sleeping parents like us. But the notion kept recurring, could we live without a telly?

We watched it sporadically – the odd box set here and there. But the truth was, we were tired of arranging our living space to incorporate this electrical device. And once Arlo started marching into the living room demanding to watch *Paw Patrol* for the hundredth time in a day, we started to think seriously about it.

Could we do it? Will people think we're weird? Do we care?

At three years old, Arlo lived most of his life with chronic ear pain. Do you know how that feels? Ear and tooth pain have a very debilitating effect and, unfortunately, his condition was misdiagnosed – meaning he suffered greatly. When you've been up six times during the night, every night, to comfort him while he screams in agony, let me just say, there's not a lot of energy left for building blocks or Lego.

We survived the first eighteen months before Arlo knew what the strange black object attached to the wall was. I think The Wife was reading some book on raising less annoying tech-addicted kids or something at the time. Anyhow, we played a lot of music and spent our time interacting with Arlo through play and the telly just wasn't used during the day.

He'd look up at it.

I'd watch his mind ticking away.

 Not quite a mirror, not a toy.

'What is dat, Daddy?'

'Never mind, Son. Go back to being cute.'

Slowly but surely, as the relentless ear infections dominated our lives, it became a tool – one utilised in emergencies in the middle of the night or when needing a moment's peace so I could, I don't know, wash the dishes, tidy the living room, and sit quietly facing the wall! Maybe The Wife could plan some lessons at the dining room table without those sticky little hands clambering all over her and the laptop!

So, we gave in. We smashed the emergency glass, retrieved the remote control, and put on the biggest regret of my life – *Paw Patrol*. That song still plays within the deep recesses of my mind... I can hear it now, *Paw Patrol, Paw Patrol,* be there on the double... stop it, stop it! Let me live! Pull yourself together, and force it back into the abyss with the opening soundtrack from *Friends* goddammit!

One hour became two. Once a day became three times. In the end, there didn't seem to be a moment when the telly wasn't on. The house had never been cleaner! His health would improve but then the weather would get worse. We had to stay in and wait for a delivery. I needed to fix something; there was always a reason to switch it on and he became a full-blown telly addict. Creating a whole new problem. Arlo would come thundering down the stairs, all blurry-eyed and chubby. A bottle of milk in one hand, something sticky in the other.

'*Paw Patrol.*'

'Why don't we play for a bit, Pudding Chops?'

He'd look at me like I was the biggest dick head to ever walk the Earth.

'*PAW PATROL*, NOW.'

I love that boy but there was a thought creeping into my mind; could we give him back somehow? Offer him to science maybe? Ove was still a few months away from birth, maybe we could put all our energies into the new one and put this snotty-nosed telly addict down to a failed experiment?

The Wife disagreed. The Boy stayed.

This meant a change was inevitable. I had to find a way to parent without relying on the television whenever I was tired or needed to complete my dad chores. I was sick of watching him stare at the screen - literally expressionless and open-mouthed.

'Fancy going to the park, Arlo?'

'Nah. Don't interrupt me until lunch.'

Three years old and already done with play! Once, the mere mention of the park, even in passing conversation would result in him flying out the door with his wellies on, but he didn't want to go anywhere or do anything. It was my duty to get tough. Tough but fair. The next morning when he came downstairs, there was a blanket over the telly.

'It's broken, Son.'

The easiest lie I've ever told.

Were you expecting some type of holistic approach? Maybe a bribe to comfort him? Nope. I unplugged the television; told him it was broken, and then sold it a few days later. We could live without it too. He was devastated. He screamed. Threw himself to the floor. Bit his fingers in protest. He wanted to get my tools out of the garage and fix it.

'Some things can't be fixed, Son.'

Absolutely true and a good life lesson to learn, I reckon.

Without the telly to rely on, I began taking note of his behaviour. What triggers reminded him the television wasn't there. How tiredness pushed his thoughts towards technology. I saw how easily I'd been saying yes and turning it on. I'd played my part in this, but I was motivated to make it right.

It took three days to wean him off. He got angry when he remembered it was no longer there. He became upset. Threw stuff,

96

and generally become very unpleasant to be around. Then, it was like a button had been pushed and he was back to himself.

We read together more, listened to music, and played instruments. I found games and toys that interested him again, and I lowered my expectations concerning my ability to parent and complete my dad chores at the same time.

Then Ove arrived. Desperation eventually followed as he developed into a sleep thief and I compromised by reintroducing some technology back into our lives. Just a small portable DVD player. A harmless, easy-to-manage, portable DVD player.

Now we have two addicts demanding to watch *Paw Patrol!*

(We lasted two years without the telly before buying another one. It wasn't because of the annoying kids in the end. It was after we'd shared a delightful stomach bug with the boys, and in between running to the toilet to let loose or puking not so quietly into a bowl in the corner, we spent most of the days in one stinky bedroom, dehydrated, bored, and huddled around that tiny portable DVD player watching an array of kids' films. Once the life returned to my body and I dared to wee standing up again, I said sod it, we're getting a telly. And yet again, I hate it.)

Co-Sleeping with Two

The thought of having a second child in the bed with us produces a twitchy, shuddery, I can't bare it, please not again kind of reaction within me. Outwardly I just smile when The Wife says things like "It's going to be amazing, snuggling next to our two babies all night."

One part of me understands that warm feeling she's evoking because when Arlo's not clawing at her boobs, screaming for milk, waking every fifty minutes, thrashing around, or slapping me in the face with his big fleshy arm in the middle of the night, while he dictates who has any space in the bed – in the rare few moments when he's not doing that, yeah, it's quite pleasurable.

My main concern is space. We already gave up sleeping on a bed and opted for sheepskin rugs on the floor. Sounds a bit Viking-like but believe me, it's good for posture and we love it... now. It was a tough sell though. The Wife was not happy with the idea. There'd been a few issues with beds and mattresses in the past.

Possibly my fault.

We'd spent hundreds on different styles of mattresses, and I could not get comfortable on any of them. The last one we tried was some super-duper springy thing with a thin memory foam layer which seemed to finally hit the spot but on the second night, I realised if I continued sleeping on that mattress, I was going to be crippled for life.

'At last. We've finally got the right one,' The Wife said as we read side by side in bed.

'Hmm mm.'

Out of the corner of my eye, I saw The Wife place her book down on her lap. I turned a page from *Life of Pi*, nervously, praying to the **Almighty** for a change in subject. Please change the subject! Don't ask me about the mattress.

'What?' She asked.

'I hate it I hate it I hate it I hate it I hate it!'

'Oh for fu... you said you liked it.'

'I lied because we'd had sex and I could've been lying on a pile of broken bricks and been comfy.'

'I give up. You truly are the Princess and the Pea.'

'I can't help it.'

'So, what are we supposed to do now?'

'I've been doing a bit of research and... this might seem a little extreme.'

'Oh my god, what is it?'

'Well, the bed's not really big enough for us when Arlo's in it as well, and with another one on the way how about this... no bed?'

Words are insufficient for the way she looked at me at that moment.

I was prepared to fight for my right to comfort. Some key advantages to sleeping on the floor were as follows:

- The baby couldn't fall out of bed.
- We would have the equivalent of a King Size bed without the cost.
- No annoying wooden plinths to smack your shins on when drunk.
- Cats couldn't shit under it.
- I would stop moaning. Hopefully. Probably.

'There's one tiny issue all the bloggers seem unanimous on though?' I continued.

'Go on.'

'The first three nights are apparently a bit...'

'What?'

'Horrendous. But on the fourth night, the discomfort vanishes as your body adapts.'

'So let's get this straight. You want to remove the expensive bed and sleep on the floor?'

'Not on the floor exactly. Sheep-skin rugs.'

That was the tipping point. The Wife's eyes darted from side to side as electrical signals in her brain fired from one synapse to another. Her body went into shock. Unable to move. The expression on her face appeared to be one of mild disgust mixed with confusion. Have you ever smelt one of your farts and wondered how something so utterly vile can come from your own body? You look around the room hoping to blame it on a dying dog as your brain struggles to understand the situation. You don't have a dog. You're alone. The fart is yours.

That expression stayed on The Wife's face even after I'd kissed her goodnight on the cheek and turned the light off.

Becca ended up getting a very expensive bed for a teenager and we found our way onto the sheep-skin rugs on the floor. The first three days were horrendous, as we had been told. For three nights I pretended it wasn't that bad. The Wife was not so accommodating. A suitcase had appeared in the room on the fourth night before we went to sleep, and half the contents of my wardrobe were stuffed inside. The message was very clear. This was the Princess and the Pea's final hurrah.

Hallelujah! The bloggers were right. The fourth night was amazing. Even Arlo seemed to have a slightly better night than usual. In the morning the suitcase was gone and The Wife liked me again.

'I told you it would be okay,' I said. Possibly a bit smug.

'Let's not get too excited just yet Miss Pea. It's not as if we haven't been here before.'

Fair point.

When the sheep-skin rugs were spread out on the floor with a blanket and huge sheet over them, the space was much larger than a double bed. Had we finally found the perfect co-sleeping solution?

No. As it turns out the more space you give a kid, the more it'll take. We have met other co-sleeping parents and the general consensus is, the children ask for their own space naturally around the age of four. Arlo's two and a bit and there's another one on the way. I really don't think I can wait that long. He's showing zero desire to fly the nest and sleep on his own.

I bought one of those tent thingies from Ikea to go over the top of his bed, so it looks like a cool den. But nothing. Within an hour he's out of it and pounding along the landing towards our room where he then spends the night wriggling, kicking and moaning his way through the night.

Can we really cope with another one in the bed?

Like it or not I've had to accept this situation because the alternative means one of us getting out of bed dozens of times a night to deal with him. Or the old-school approach of controlled crying which, no matter how many times he slaps and kicks me in the night, doesn't appeal. He clearly needs our support. When he reaches out for me in the night and whispers "Dadda," or leans over in the morning and kisses me on the cheek, it fills me with love that I somehow turn into strength which gets me through another day.

But two of them... shudder!

Conversation with A Teenager

It's Friday evening and I walk into the kitchen ready to open a bottle of red. The Wife's choosing a film to watch, and the boys are in bed before 7 pm which makes this a great night. Becca's making smashed avocado on toast and wearing her comfy clothes which have more stains on them than a washing powder advert. Her hair's tied up and she's watching *Friends* on her phone; all the tell-tale signs she's staying in.

'You staying in tonight?' I ask anyway.

'Yeah,' she says. 'Just chilling.'

Told you.

'That's not like you.'

'I know. I'm tired.'

'We're just about to watch a film if you fancy it? We can watch something shit just for you.'

'Arr, thanks. I might do later.'

'It's nice to have you here on a Friday. We never usually see you.'

'I know.'

I swiftly open the wine and grab two glasses.

'Did you get the washing out of the machine?' she asks.

If I had a pound coin for every time I've asked her that very question, I'd be swimming like Scrooge McDuck now. Diving headfirst into a pile of coins.

'Seriously? I'm literally about to sit down.'

She doesn't bother to look at me. Chandler Bing is about to do something funny.

'But I need some clothes for tomorrow.'

'You've got loads of clothes.'

'I need a red top.'

'A red top? That's so silly.'

'Can you sort it please?'

'Can't you do it?'

'I'm making some food.'

She pauses *Friends,* turns, and gives me a look of pure helplessness.
A *but I'm so tired look.* Her bottom lip doesn't exactly tremble
because she's too good, but it's there. Just a whiff. In her defence,
she's just started a new job. She's knackered. I'm not. What the hell?

'Right, I'll do it now.'

'Thanks.'

Friends back on. End of conversation. I take the wine into the
lounge and place it on the small table which has only one purpose

in existence; to look after my wine and snacks and make sure I don't have to stretch very far to get it.

'I've got to put the washing out,' I tell The Wife.

'Er. Why? Leave it.'

'Becca wants to put some in.'

'Get her to do it.'

'I tried but she's... never mind, I'm doing it. Back in ten.'

In record time I arrive back in the lounge just as Becca blows past me like a hurricane of smells and hair, wearing a bright red top and chatting on a video call.

'I'm staying out tonight. See you later.'

The door opens and slams shut.

We don't see or hear from her for three days.

A Lockdown Story

Depression almost wrapped its dark tentacles around my mind recently. It's happened before. Many times in fact, but I'm taking steps to minimise the chances of it occurring again because I really like being happy. I've curated a wellness toolkit which keeps me on the right side of positivity.

Mostly.

Sometimes I forget where I've put the toolkit, resulting in several days wandering around the house looking under discarded toys, the sofa, inside the wine bottles, in every place but within me where it lives. When I find it and look inside the feeling is on par with being a kid and opening a discarded birthday card you had considered to have zero chance of financial gain, only to discover a tenner inside.

Once I begin examining the contents of the toolkit I remember why I have one, and the negative path I've been on becomes clear.

I've been stuck in a cycle. I can step out of it. I can remember.

The tools appear like old friends who smile warmly.

'Hey, Fresh Air, how you doing?'

'You've been smoking again,' Fresh Air says a little judgementally.

'Yes, but I was thinking about you the whole time.'

I take a few deep breaths and remember.

Next comes out an old, confused, haggard-looking friend who needs a little extra care. I rest the tool down on a small rug, made by tribeswomen from some exotic part of the world, with crystals I have no idea how to use, and I light an incense stick.

I squeeze Meditation's shoulder reassuringly.

'Have we met?' Meditation hesitates. 'I recognise your face.'

'Yes, old friend.'

We smile at each other. The sun bursts through the window covering the room with a bright light at precisely the right moment.

'Do I have to go back in the box?' Meditation asks.

'Let's not talk about that right now.'

We sit peacefully and remember.

The tools don't only help me sustain a happy life in the present, they've aided me with retracing depressive threads from my past which have had a profound effect on my thought processes and well-being. Having a supportive partner and being a dad has been the catalysts for great change within me.

But it's come at a cost of forcing these threads out into the open and confronting what's at the end. If you ever reach his point and you've not considered vital tools like talk therapy, positive lifestyle changes, or self-reflection, you could end up repeating the cycle over and over.

It gets harder to return to that sweet place called denial once you begin using the tools so be warned. Change is inevitable. Depression is sneaky!

It's an opportunist. And once I'd made the subconscious decision to dropkick some tools back into the toolkit, because I tricked myself into thinking I could take a well-earned break, depression was waiting in the shadows; hungry and ready to pounce.

But Lockdown 2022 was not a normal life experience. I think we can say, without question, it was nothing like we could have prepared for. I won't share my opinions on the politics of the Lockdown, but I will say this - it felt like a holiday at first.

Sparkling wine might as well have poured straight from the tap to my glass. Which put me in a delightful mood until about 6 pm when I had to reignite that buzz with a vodka tonic. It became a bit of a pattern of behaviour. Nowhere to go, unlimited food and drink and amazing sunshine every day.

Sounds like the dictionary term for an all-inclusive holiday to me.

The sun has always been a trigger for consuming more alcohol in the UK. It's our blood rite. But as Lockdown dragged on, I started to notice a dependency emerging. One that began to sour my mood and affect the way I was parenting.

It's not like I drank wine all day, every day and completely ignored my kids. I usually mustered a "hello" to them over breakfast as they helped themselves to whatever was in the fridge and cupboards and danced on the table naked. I'd grab a block of cheese and some oak cakes and just get the hell out of there.

On proactive days when we managed to get our act together, we'd take advantage of the Lockdown measures and enjoy our allocated daily outdoor exercise time. We strolled around local parks, trails and paths filled with litter and dog shit.

That was depressing enough.

We had to think outside the box. Find new ways to enjoy the outdoors without the use of the play areas which were closed. We started den making, bird spotting (God forgive me) and a hundred variations of hide and seek. It was a lot of fun. But it was weird because most places were empty and quiet when they should have been lively with people. There was this feeling that home was better than out.

At home we had water fights, paddling pools, and lots of bubbles. We had ice creams and ice lollies. Every meal or snack felt like it was part of an all-you-can-eat buffet. I was using white crusty bread loaded with butter instead of cutlery to shovel several forms of salad, meat and dippy things into my constantly open mouth. Cheese, of course, crackers, cake and fruit smoothies. Chocolate in a hundred different forms seemed to appear magically in my hand. I was getting cases of wine delivered every two weeks rather than once a year!

We discovered a love for vodka orange because it made The Wife and I feel light and giggly. Oh, and cider because when it's hot you just got to have a cider. It's the law.

All this consumption. All these earthy pleasures designed to give me a quick fix. A short relief from the global fear being shoved down our throats. The fear. The lockdowns. The boredom. The consumption! All accumulated into a moment of clarity once I remembered where my toolkit was.

The Wife and I came to an understanding - the drink needed to be put back into its place. Two nights a week maximum. We returned to intermittent fasting, which we both value, and the only treats allowed in the house had to be home-baked. No more easy-to-reach sugary snacks. No more tipsy, easy-to-manipulate parents either!

The kids were mortified.

They couldn't understand why the holiday was over.

They were loving it. At first, they were confused about schools closing and the restrictions. But they become accustomed, like we did, to living this all-inclusive holiday lifestyle. Everything changed so quickly. One day the kids had school, friends, and routines and the next it ended. Replaced with this strange new life based within the confines of the home with their watery-eyed parents who now had a sudden tendency to say yes to everything and wore the same stained shorts and t-shirts every day while listening to *Fleetwood Mac* very loudly on repeat.

The motivation for change came once we realised the boys were morphing into rule-phobic wild beasts addicted to ice lollies and the third Aladdin movie no one's seen, ever! The realisation coincided with lockdown restrictions being eased which gave us more freedom to travel further afield. It helped with the monotony of trying to make the visit to the same park, for the seventh time in a week, more interesting.

Gaining this slight freedom raised all of our positivity levels and for me personally, I was able to look rationally at my own mental health and see how I'd locked my wellness toolkit away with my running shoes and the ability to locate water instead of wine.

Surviving the Summer

I've always loved the summer. More than any other season. Crusty skin peeling off my Irish heritage white nose and forehead. Dealing with the constant threat of running out of ice cubes. All the windows open all the time. Duvets in the cupboard. Heatwaves that last weeks. The smell of freshly cut grass. Water fights. Long days. All that stuff. The Wife sees things differently. She's the kind of positive person who appreciates each season.

'All the seasons have a special role to play. Spring is about renewal and...'

'Let me stop you there, Babe, I don't care.'

I'm not interested. I'll take a little bit of autumn and the best bits of spring, but those long dark days of winter just drag. Maybe I'd enjoy it more if we hibernated; months spent getting fat on barbecued food washed down with Swedish mixed berry ciders, made from crystal-clear freshwater springs which are in fact melting glaciers! Each day from the beginning of March right through to the end of August, gorging on high-fat greasy foods and sugary everythingz.

After August we should just hibernate. Gain loads of weight during the summer months then just go to bed. Six-pack stomachs are for losers because the fatter you are the more desirable you become to skinny members of the opposite sex who will need to rely on licking your salty sweat to survive the winter months locked in your bedroom with a portable loo and a couple of Amazon Fire Tablets.

The mornings were the best when I was a kid and got even better in my twenties. I'd open my eyes and immediately know it was going to be a good day. I'd stretch. Scratch a bit. Pretend to meditate for five minutes, then open the curtains fully and embrace the day.

There was always an air of possibility about what lay ahead. Not that I actually achieved much but the feeling was always there. I'd watch the human activity outside, already in full swing as if it was lunchtime. Derek the flat cap guy washing his car, again! Kids chalking huge cock and ball motifs on the pavements, cats motionless on a fence waiting to torment and dismember a pigeon. The sky, cloudless and blue, stretched as far as the eye could see. And that smell. That glorious freshly cut grass smell. Amazing.

Work was even fun back then in the 90s for me because it was with a group of mates. We'd all go to the pub at lunch to have a few pints. Returning to work forty-five minutes later - red-faced and smiley. Eager to smash out the next couple of hours of production so we could escape as soon as humanly possible. After work, we'd head straight back to the pub where there was the very real possibility of getting extremely messy until silly O'clock in the morning.

After a few stolen hours, the rude alarm clock would sound and I'd swiftly press the snooze button. Fifteen minutes to get up and ready, I can get that down to five! I never went back to sleep of course, this just gave my mind enough time to replay the previous day's events in a reasonably coherent order. And a quick download of all the utter shit I'd be chatting about!

Then the best bit...

Lying there focused on the glass of water on the bedside cabinet. Always out of reach physically and mentally. My brain screaming for moisture. Cracked lips and a tongue wrapped in concrete. When body and consciousness got it together and I could muster the cognitive power to reach over and take it, to quench that thirst, then it was usually time to get up and in all likelihood repeat!

Now when I feel that early morning humidity and open my eyes, I see two young children leaning over me like menacing shadows of expectation.

'Can we get up now?' Arlo asks.

'Give me a second, Son. I've just woken up.'

Three seconds...

'Can we get up now?' they both demand.

'Okay, Boys. Let's be quiet, don't want to wake your fake sleeping mum, do we?'

She doesn't move an inch. She's a pro.

Summer now consists of locating shade and water during the day and surviving with two sleep thieves, through the night. And the night doesn't come at the usual strict time of 7 pm does it? Oh no. The kids don't believe that it's bedtime.

'But It's still light?' Arlo says.

'It does that in the summer.'

'I want to play outside.'

'Mummy and Daddy want to drink wine.'

'Me and Ove want to watch a film.'

'You just said you wanted to play outside.'

Long pause... He considers his options.

'Here's the deal. Let us watch one more film.'

'And what? Where's the bit I want?'

Long pause...

'I'll give you 10p.'

'Bed. Now.'

Longer days ruin our watertight bedtime routine which is a massive problem for me because I don't want to see any kid's face between the hours of 7 pm and 7 am. Evening time is adult time. For doing grown-up stuff like tidying up the kitchenware that finds its way into the garden, littered amongst every pillow, cushion, and blanket you own. And toys. Lots and lots of spikey toys that love sticking in your bare, I'm so grounded right now, feet.

After those jobs, you unload the dishwasher for the fifth time then guess what? You flipping load it again, wipe the sides, locate ten more used glasses scattered around the lounge and wash them in the sink. You take the washing off the line (three lots dried in a day, get in!) open the wine, get the snacks ready and chill in the garden with your partner for a few blessed minutes before the children wake up screaming because they're too hot, overtired, bla, bla, bla.

In the end, it's not worth staying up so we go to bed and bring them into our room. It's too much hassle getting up thirty times a night to attend to their woes. So, we end up with four humans fighting for a cold patch in one sleeping space. And the kids seem to enjoy the pain and suffering for some reason. They thrive off it. I'm constantly having to peel Arlo's sweaty leg off my own every couple of minutes, tearing it off like soggy velcro while pleading with him to please stop touching me.

The Wife stares expressionless up at the ceiling as the industrial-sized fans blow warm air into her face from several directions while Ove tries to claw the final droplets of milk from her crusty nipples. She already went through this with Arlo. Watching her endure it again just breaks my heart.

'I love you, Babe.' I whisper.

'This is your fault.'

'How's it my fault?'

'There's something wrong with them. This isn't normal,' she hisses back.

'Whoa, chill out. I know there's something wrong with them but why automatically assume it's from my side of the gene pool?'

'Becca never did any of this. No one else's kids do this! All night. Every night.'

'Gentle parenting.'

'What?'

'I blame it on gentle parenting, we should have-'

'We should have what? Beat them?'

'I'm just saying-'

'Well don't.'

122

A long pause.

'I meant controlled crying. We should have done that controlled crying thing.'

The way she sucks in air through her nostrils tells me that was the wrong thing to say.

'Go away, now.'

I tiptoe out of the room and never mention it again.

When the World Made Sense

Remember when Shrek wished for a single day without any responsibility? A day he could return to his free-spirited youth, running half naked around his swamp with a Porn Star Martini at 11 am on a Wednesday morning after a busy night terrifying the simple folk. A single day when having a PIP (poo in peace) without kids banging at the door was his basic right.

He just wanted a day *when the world made sense.* His words.

Shrek looked around and recognised only predictability and routine. The reality of parenthood, sleep deprivation, and pairing

124

socks overshadowed the positive aspects of being in the present with his family. His discontentment grew until he eventually snapped!

I totally get it.

Imagine having one day to live your old life again. It's not like Shrek asked for much. One measly day. Parenting beat the imagination out of him. Twenty-four hours released from the shackles of responsibility does sound appealing. Most parents I speak to would probably just sleep – wake up the next day refreshed and say it was worth it. I once thought they were losers. Party poopers. The kind of people that won't have another beer because it's a "school night!"

But now I get it. Oh, how I get it now!

How do you make *your* wishes? Do you grit your teeth, squeeze your eyes shut and plead with the almighty to intervene? Do you make big wishes? Or are you the quiet type muttering almost insignificant wishes under your breath regularly because you don't really expect anyone to help?

However you do it, I warn you, be careful what you wish for. One day the planets might align and grant it. And that could be the beginning of a long and painful period in your life you just aren't mentally equipped to handle.

I know this because it happened to me.

One dark winter's night many moons ago, a sentence was uttered. An empathetic gesture which was taken literally and most definitely shouldn't have been!

'I wish I could help more with the bedtime routine,' I said quietly whilst gently shaking my head in a show of shared frustration.

This was so obviously a simple show of emotional support. But there was trickery afoot on this cold dark night as my words caught a draught and echoed loudly off the walls.

"I wish I could help more with the bedtime routine!"

The lights flickered.

The Wife raised her head. Her pale face was obscured by the greasy matted hair streaked across it. Her eyes... those tired red eyes. Those desperate eyes. I'll never forget them. That mixture of suffering, pity, and something I'm unable to put into words. I'd made this wish before but this time the twitching and her right hand crushing the arm of the chair told me it had been granted.

'Yeeeessssss.'

'Erm, what was that, Dear?'

I headed swiftly towards the kitchen.

'Need to put some olive oil in my ears, I'm going deaf.'

I wriggled my finger inside my ear for effect.

The kitchen door was only a metre away. The light behind it felt safe. Welcoming. Like everything from the past thirty seconds would be erased if I could just get to it. Get behind it into the warm glow of safety. But I didn't move quickly enough. I blinked and she was in front of me. Her hot primal breath overpowered my personal space.

'You can help with the bedtime routine,' she said.

She stepped even closer.

'Mooore.'

Cold sweat ran down my spine. My balls ached. I felt sick.

Ove, now resembling a wild creature rather than a baby, looked at me with his fierce blue eyes and soaking wet everything. I reached a loving hand towards **it**, hoping to offer it some comfort as **it** squirmed in The Wife's arms but only rage and tears sprung from every atom of **its** being. Before I could back away The Wife had already unloaded **it** onto me.

Silence filled the air. That deafening silence that replaces chaos. Ear ringing silence!

I looked down at the wild creature. We shared a psychic connection. A knowing. We both knew life was never going to be the same again. I started to panic as my new reality merged with the old. I wanted to tell her that I'd opened wine. That I was about to watch a film and chill out. How I'm a better daytime parent.

It didn't matter.

There was a flash of movement to my side as the lounge door crashed open and a dark shape moved through it out of the room. I raced with Ove towards the hallway, stopping at the threshold and peering into the darkness.

'Babe,' I whispered.

I patted the wall searching for the light switch but hesitated when I found it.

'Where are-'

Ove kicked out, straightening his body flatter than a plank! I accidentally pushed the light switch before dropping to my knees, catching him in the process. I rolled onto my back as the dull LED bulb illuminated the stairway.

I couldn't see her at first, but I could hear strange crunching and slurping noises. As my eyes adjusted, I finally saw The Wife under the stairs devouring snacks from Arlo's nursery bag.

'Easy now, eeeasy.'

She leapt onto the bannister, turned, hissed, and then pounced up the stairs, taking several at a time. The bedroom door slammed shut. There was a heavy thud, some incoherent muttering then a noise so uncanny I have no simile to liken it to – I can only surmise that it was the sound of snoring.

I looked down at my son. I loved this boy. I had no problem getting him to sleep during the day. How hard can it be to do it at night?

Six months later...

I have no concept of time... of self... I often consider crying... I only sweat under one armpit, never both, and he uses my scabby nipple as a comforter. These could be the final coherent words I manage to send from my brain to my... erm, what were we talking about?

The Snip

'I don't wanna.' I plead

'Condoms it is then,' The Wife replies.

'There must be another option?'

'Nothing.'

'How about that temperature thing?'

'Oh yeah, I'll check my temperature before we have sex then hope for the best. Good one.'

'But the snip seems so drastic. So final.'

'It's a minor incision. You'll be in and out in half an hour.'

'But...'

'What?'

'Nuffin.'

'What is it?'

'It's stupid.'

'I'm prepared for that.'

'It's two things.'

'Give me the lesser of the two first.'

'Okay. What if it comes out weird? What if it's disgusting?'

'I have some news for you, Husband, it's already disgusting.'

'You know what I mean?'

'I know exactly what you mean and unless you get fitted with some chocolate sauce-producing balls it's always going to be disgusting.'

'What if it's all thin and weird?'

'Rather than thick and gloopy? I'd say that was an improvement.'

'I knew you'd be insensitive. That's why I didn't want to say anything.'

'I'm being as sensitive as I possibly can considering I gave birth to your second child less than a week ago.'

'It's not coming across as sensitivity.'

'I'm not going to indulge in this ridiculousness.'

'It's not ridiculous to me. Imagine having an operation-'

'Minor procedure.'

'An operation which suddenly changes the colour of your blood?'

'Why would I want to change the colour of my blood?

'You don't, that's the point.'

'You've lost me.'

'You don't get it.'

'You've got that right.'

'I'm trying to talk about a genuine fear and you're laughing at me.'

'Trust me, I'm not laughing.'

Silence.

'I'm sorry if you think I'm laughing. I'm not. I just don't think you're being very rational.'

'I don't think I am either. I'm having a lot of crazy thoughts.'

'What was the second thing?'

'Ay?'

'You said there were two things on your mind.'

'Oh. Promise you won't laugh?'

'I'll try my best.'

'I can't shake this idea that it'll stop me from... erm...'

'What?'

'From you know?'

'I have no idea.'

'That it's going to be like cutting off the source of my horny powers. Once I've been snipped, I won't feel the urge for sexy time anymore. I'll end up being like those other blokes who would rather play five-a-side footy with their mates. Or worse, I'll get one of those chairs and sit for hours playing shooting games online with a headset on. There I said it. If I get the snip that's going to happen. Is that what you want?'

'I'll take my chances. I'm booking the appointment.'

And that was that.

Note to dads:

It was alright in the end. Relatively painless. There was a strange smell and a few tugging sensations. The doctor was very gentle. Afterwards, I felt like I'd done a thousand sit-ups and tight underwear is the way to go. After a week or so I conducted a small experiment of my own and, as it turns out, apart from a tiny bit of blood, all was still thick and gloopy and I'm still as horny as a teenager.

A Lockdown Story

I didn't know this pre-kids, but I was built for play. I'm that guy rocking a headscarf and colourful beads while the boys shuffle around in mama's high heels. I take hide and seek very seriously, remaining hidden, breath held, till the very death or at least until bursting for a wee. I allow mess. Lots of mess. It's going to happen anyway, so I get on board and enjoy it.

There's something liberating about dragging the folded towels and sheets from the shelves, adding them to a huge pile of duvets and pillows in the middle of the bedroom, and then spending half a day chucking the boys through the air onto it. They don't get bored and neither do I.

When Lockdown was first introduced, we felt well-equipped to handle it. Our house is designed for play: Black board-painted walls, and dens everywhere! Art corners and a back garden stuffed with tuff trays, water play equipment and a mud kitchen. It felt like an extended weekend. Later nights. More telly than usual. Time to blow the dust off that *Learn Spanish in A Week* CD. Wine with tea? Wine with lunch more like. Add some glorious weather into the mix and that extended weekend evolved into an early summer holiday but with two differences:

- You couldn't go anywhere further than your local green space.
- You couldn't socialise.

It didn't take long before the cracks showed. Parenting 24/7 was a tough slog. We'd fallen into the trap of overusing the word "yes." It was *sooo* easy at first. The kids were loving it. But the holiday spirit ended once we reintroduced the word "no." The atmosphere quickly soured. Patience and tolerance were shelved. Play was a chore. We seemed to run out of ideas. So, as most parents will understand, we turned to the telly more and more. The good old third parent. The bringer of so much pleasure with a side order of addiction!

The third parent gave us a little peace. But it broke the boys. They malfunctioned, unable to focus on anything but the telly. They suffered from a lack of coordination – ice lollies in the eye, juice straight onto their sticky bellies. Food scattered about in all directions. When they bothered to speak it was bossy and Neolithic.

'Dad, we hungry.'

'You've only just finished your third breakfast, Son. Look down, most of it's on your chest.'

Eyes fixed on the third parent.

'We hungry now. Dad, get food now.'

It wasn't even 10 am!

'I'll make you both lunch in an hour. Butties, crisps, and some chopped-up apples. A mini picnic.'

'We want crisps and chopped-up apples now. Dad, get or we make you sorry.'

And they did make us sorry.

A lot.

We had to get tough which meant turning off the telly and becoming active loving parents again. And with our boys, that means play. Lots of play. If they are not sufficiently entertained in some form or another, they begin ripping wallpaper off or seriously try to hurt each other.

Drawing on paper is not enough, you need to build a den (which takes an hour) from the hundred Amazon boxes piled at the front door, so they can decorate it using all the paints, all the crayons, and snot before destroying it after five minutes.

Then they stand there like, *now what?*

It was exhausting.

The Wife and I would tag each other in like-beaten wrestlers. I'd take the 6 am till 12 pm slot and she'd have the little beasts until teatime. I'd arrive at the baby gate, bruised, sweating and dazed. I'd hang onto the gate then raise my hand in the air and wait for that slap of the hand – the tag – that sweet release from the relentless pummelling of my mind, body and patience by the little beasts.

Then it would come. Tag!

The Wife, freshly dressed and watered, with a can-do look in her eye, would slap herself around the face several times, stamp her feet then bunny hop over the baby gate into the pit of insanity. She'd grip my ankles and push me headfirst over the gate to relative safety. Never taking her eyes from the pile of cushions in the centre of the room, knowing a naked beast could attack with a large wooden spoon at any moment.

'What're you doing now? Writing? Painting the bathroom? Learning Spanish? Upskilling?' The Wife would ask.

Me? I was already getting my supplies together.

'I'm off to the front garden with a bottle of Prosecco and some cheese.'

'But it's barely midday.'

'I know. See ya!'

I'd leap from the kitchen window onto the boiling hot metal vehicle below, using my flabby body and a packet of Edam cheese slices to protect my champagne flute and cheap Prosecco from the impact.

24/7 parenting, with nowhere new to go, and no one to see, created a tangible strain inside our home. We all felt it. As lockdown eased, we travelled beyond our local area, exploring woods with streams to paddle in and hills to climb. This occupied us for most of the day and was the turning point that broke the monotony of lockdown. We found a way to balance yes and no again but it was tough for a while.

Really tough!

But some key lessons were learnt: Drinking sparkling wine before lunch is not the best motivator long-term. You can't rely on the telly to parent your kids (Who knew?) and Amazon boxes do actually come in handy.

Downstairs

5 am: I know he's awake. He's huffing, puffing, and rolling around in the covers like a baby crocodile ripping a gazelle to pieces. He pulls the duvet off me completely, exposing my cold battered body. I try to stay as fake asleep as possible and pull the cover back onto my side of the bed while making "I'm still asleep" groany noises.

It's gone quiet. No movement. You never know, he might go back to sleep. **Ha!**

5:05 am: He's literally breathing down my ear. I can taste his breath inside my skull.

5:09 am: It's gone quiet again. I take a chance and open one crusty eye. He's staring right at me. Shit!

'Dad.'

This pointless game is over.

'Good morning, Son.'

'Can we go downstairs and watch that film?'

'I used to consider 5 am as night-time, you know?'

'The one when the mum and dad die when the tiger kills them and the baby cries in the treehouse.'

'I don't think it's a tiger.'

'And then he lives with the monkeys.'

'Gorillas.'

'What's it called again?'

'Tarzan.'

'That's it. Can we watch it?'

'No. Go back to sleep.'

He leans over my face and shares with me a continuous stream of thoughts, bargaining strategies, beliefs, and reasons why he should be allowed to watch Tarzan.

5:10 am: 'But, Dad!'

'No.'

5:11 am: His little brother enters the bedroom.

5:12 am: Downstairs watching Tarzan.

Dirty Talk

It's a rare, peaceful night. The boys are sound asleep. Completely wiped out before I'd even finished reading the second book. They haven't woken up yet and it's nearly 10 pm! That's a record. God, it feels good to sit here under faded lights with a glass of red, an endless supply of crisps and The Wife.

I turn slightly to The Wife and smile. She smiles back.

'I don't remember the last time we watched a full film all the way through without having to check on the boys a hundred times,' I point out.

'I know. It usually takes about four hours to watch one film.'

'This is nice.'

I smile at The Wife.

'It is.'

She smiles back.

We watch the rest of the film, drink our wine, and munch our crisps, without being disturbed. Fifteen minutes after the film ends and they still haven't woken up. The baby monitor crackles away in the corner of the room, oddly quiet for the first time in its existence.

This is uncharted territory. The second bottle of wine's been drunk.

We can't open a third. Can we? That's crazy talk.

'Is that all the wine?'

The Wife shakes her empty glass for effect.

'It's the last of the bottle, not the last of the wine.'

I watch The Wife complete a risk assessment in her head. She's calculating whether it's possible to throw caution to the wind and get super pissed. Can we stay up later than 11 pm? Are we pushing it? Will the kids wake up screaming the moment we open the next bottle? Will one of them suddenly develop croup? One will definitely wake up during the night, so how drunk is irresponsible drunk?

We deserve one late night though, don't we?

It's Saturday tomorrow, they can watch the telly all day, and eat rubbish while we lie in bed dehydrated and smelly.

Once she's completed the calculation, her expression informs me it's time for bed.

'We better not,' she says.

I take her empty glass and place it on the floor. I squeeze up close, gently push her back into the warmth of the sofa and begin to kiss her neck.

'One day, do you know what I'm going to do?' I whisper into her ear.

'What?'

'I'm going to find someone to babysit those boys for a full night.'

'Stop teasing.'

'I mean it. Then, I'm going to book us into a fancy hotel.'

'Yeah.'

'An old one with a four-poster bed. A massive one.'

'Then what?'

She strokes my back and pulls me tighter as I continue to gently kiss her neck and earlobe.

'We'll pay for an early check-in and a chilled bottle of sparkling to be waiting in the room.'

'And some chocolates?'

'Yeah, hundreds of chocolates.'

'And we'll drink the wine and eat the chocolates,' The Wife says all breathy. 'Then...?'

'Then I'll pull back the heavy duvet - guide you over to the bed and undress you slowly.'

'Then?'

'Then I'll pull the duvet over you, close the curtains and put a Do Not Disturb sign on the door. Then slide in behind you and sleep!'

'For how long?'

There are tears in her eyes.

'All night, baby.'

'All night?' she mouths.

'And most of the day depending on what time we check out.'

'I want it so bad.'

'I know.'

The baby monitor shrieks to life with a child's cry and reality returns. The Wife's up in a flash and heading towards the door like the amazing mum she is. She turns before exiting the room.

'I'll hold you to that, Husband.'

'It's a promise.'

A Bit of Easy

Sometimes, usually when he's tired and splattered in paint and sticky things, he thinks about what his life was like before parenthood. A life without structure. No real purpose. Except for the pursuit of drink, drugs, and short-term physical connection which all the other aspects of his life revolved around: Job, no job, new job, drink, drugs, sex, holidays, nights out, days out, weekends out! A little bit of self-care for short intense periods of time which included: Meditation, gym, healthy eating, healthy thinking, and healthy living!

The reason his mind wanders into the past, he thinks, is because there's a small part of him that's waiting for it to return. That somehow, someone is going to point out he's not a responsible adult yet and it's all been a mistake. It's like a section of his brain believes the part of himself, the bit he didn't need to share with anyone, will return and the purposeless life with no structure can continue where it left off.

But the real him, the mind behind the mind, doesn't really want that old life back. Sometimes he's just tired of being a parent. Tired of being responsible. When he looks back he knows that although life might have been lacking some depth, it was also easy. And every now and again he could do with a bit of easy. Couldn't everyone?

Don't we all need a bit of easy sometimes?

When he was a kid, being a parent seemed simple enough. Most of the adults smoked anywhere they wanted. Drank anytime they wanted. Had parties. Went on holiday without their kids. He spent a lot of time at his Grandparents with his brothers where the food on offer was usually unhealthy and delicious. Lots of meats and fatty foods, and white bread with everything! Entertainment was limited. They had a couple of videotapes to choose from which they watched over and over again but that was alright because they didn't know any better.

No one ever took the time to explain things to him. He had to keep questions inside. Family secrets trickled out over time and confused him because he had to piece bits together himself. This often left him feeling more confused, but he just had to accept it.

It's not like that for his boys. All things must rotate around his children because they don't keep things inside. They let it all out from dawn to dusk every day. All plans, actions, and most of the learning and conversation with his wife are based around their boys. They require a lot of attention. They don't seem able to just, be. External stimuli, whether that be food or entertainment, are always at the forefront of their minds.

When he was a kid, he was happy to play at the bottom of the stairs with his action figures for as long as he was allowed. For him, that was his favourite thing to do and the less adult interference the better.

He knows he shouldn't look back and compare the parenting styles from the past to his own. It was a different world in the 80s and 90s. In fact, comparing himself to anyone else is probably not helpful or necessary. Once he might have used language like, "I've made sacrifices for my boys." But now he thinks about "choices."

He and his wife have gone without a steady income. They've gone without many things. The idea of rushing around each morning, sorting breakfast, teeth, clothes, books, bags and all that stuff before scrambling out of the door and then reversing it in the evening is a painful thought for them. Sleep deprivation has shown them that it's impossible anyway.

Could they have done it differently in those early years?

On the days when he's feeling sorry for himself because he's had very little sleep, no time with his wife, zero adult fun and the boys are being argumentative or simply annoying – he takes comfort in the phrase, "This too shall pass," which reminds him to find pleasure in the little things. He knows this time is precious, he just needs reminding every now and again.

The Sperm Collector

'I think I'm pregnant.'

'Hmm mm.'

I rolled my eyes and continued searching Netflix for something new.

I knew what was coming next.

'Can you go to Morrisons and get me a test?'

I knew it.

'No.'

'Please?'

It wasn't the first time it had happened. For a woman who had already felt a child growing inside her, hi Becca, it's amazing how many times she gets wind confused with pregnancy.

'I'm going food shopping tomorrow. I'll get one then.'

'Don't you want to know whether I'm pregnant now?'

'No.'

'Babe!'

'Leave me alone. I've been looking for something to watch for about an hour. I'm going to see if I can break my record and get to two hours without finding anything. I'm very excited about it.'

I'm not sure how many pregnancy tests I purchased during those months but definitely enough to play Jenga with. I was tired of buying them. The same conversation ran through my head every time I entered the supermarket.

Me: 'Why don't I buy two?'

Mind: 'But what if she's pregnant?'

Me: 'Then I'll be stuck with an extra one we don't need.'

Mind: 'Exactly. They're not cheap.'

Me: 'I could always bring it back to the shop?'

Mind: 'Haha. You can't be arsed doing that.'

Me: 'You know me so well.'

I don't have a problem going to the shop for my lovely wife, the shop is where I buy wine. It's the fact she, maybe it's pure coincidence, though I have my doubts, always asked me while I was chilling out. Plus, I had my money on wind because of all the farting she pretended I couldn't hear or smell.

There's one more reason I believed it was a waste of time.

'Babe,' I said.

I sat up straight and put on my most serious face.

'I've never said this out loud, but I don't think I can have kids.'

She pulled a funny face and stared at me for ages.

Mind: 'She thinks you've got an STD.'

Me: 'That's impossible.'

Mind: 'Is it?'

Me: 'We've been together for years so yes.'

Mind: 'She thinks you're a freak.'

Me: 'No she doesn't.'

Mind: 'Maybe you are?'

Me: 'Will you piss off!'

She placed a supportive hand on mine.

'What makes you think that?'

I detailed, as tactfully as a husband can, a delightful little tale about many sexual partners and a total disregard for contraception. The fact none had come forward baring a small child with my undeniable charm and shit hair. I explained how I'd never received a friend request from an unknown child or mother asking me to supply school trousers and an iPhone. This evidence plus years of drink and drug use could only mean one thing.

'I'm barren.'

'Men can't be...'

The Wife squeezed my hand and spoke softly.

'You're going to have to do it in a cup.'

'Ay?'

'I'm making you an appointment at the family clinic. You're getting tested.'

"Do it in a cup." She makes it sound so easy. Just do it in a cup, with no candles, soft music or even a bath. Who did she think I was? A teenager! I thought I'd left cups, socks, pillow slips and all that behind me.

'Do I have to?'

'Yes. It's the only way to be sure.'

'Can you come with me?'

'No way.'

'Why not?'

'I have to go for a smear test on my own – you get to do this.'

'What if I can't cum.'

'I'm sure you'll power through. Like an athlete crossing the finishing line.'

As it turned out, I didn't have to stand in a poorly lit room at the doctor's romancing myself while looking through a Country Life Magazine. I was able to take the little pot home with me and complete the deed while The Wife stood outside the bedroom shouting, "Can I come in yet? I need to dry my hair." She gave me a whole ten minutes. No pressure. Luckily for me, I had eight minutes to spare. I was already avoiding my shameful reflection in the mirror by the time she barged in.

(Not really. I waved the cup of goo in her face.)

'It's still warm, touch it.'

'Piss off you dirty boy.'

A week or so later I received my results. My sperm was fine. Apparently, I had a few lazy ones not willing to take on the hazardous journey, and a healthy percentage ready to invade The Wife's inhospitable environment at any moment. There was nothing to be concerned about but a short list of suggestions was provided: No heavy drinking. Don't romance myself too often. Don't smoke crack. And with a bit of nature's will, we were good to go.

This was encouraging news. I felt positive. For The Wife, the news created more of a physical response. Basically, she couldn't keep her bloody hands off me!

At first, it was amazing.

'Right, come on,' she'd whisper.

I'd be over in a shot. Kissing, cuddling, fondling our way to the eventual orgasm. It was bliss. Lovemaking at its best. For about a month, my life was so sweet. The Wife and I were mature students at the time. She took her studies very seriously. I have a more relaxed approach. Like drinking beer before midday. Smoking spliffs with the cool kids at uni. And some days, literally doing nothing. If I was feeling adventurous I'd clean the bathroom just for fun or find other ways to procrastinate, like rearranging the furniture. Anything that kept me away from completing my assignments.

The Wife took full advantage of my willingness to avoid my studies though. Sex in the kitchen, the garage – when I least expected it. Morning, noon and night. I was living the dream.

Then one day, it all changed.

'Right, come on,' she ordered.

I slammed my laptop shut, leapt over the desk, rubbed some warmth into my hands - flipped a fresh mint into my grinning mouth and danced provocatively over to the bed like Patrick flipping Swayze. Smooth. Sexy. I leaned down and took in the sight of my beautiful wife. I placed a loving hand on her cheek and kissed her tenderly on the lips.

'No time for any of that, just get on with it.'

'Erm, seriously?'

'I've got work to do.'

Wow! What did she think I was, a piece of meat? How rude. I must admit, as I began taking my trousers off, I felt a little cheap but I love The Wife so I did what I was told.

'Okay,' I said. 'Just this once.'

I can't lie. I struggled to enjoy it. She made it worse by constantly checking her watch and tutting during the act of lovemaking. But I'm a trooper. A professional. With a lot of concentration and plenty of toe-curling, panting and butt-clenching techniques – I was able to produce the sperm.

This became the norm.

From then on, even if I was tired, or if I wanted to talk about her day, or my feelings goddamit! It didn't matter. She might as well have had a whip, cracking it on the floor around my feet.

'Perform for me.'

CRACK CRACK CRACK

'Now!'

My favourite pastime became a chore. I've never been the type to cry after sex, but it was getting close. My penis looked like it'd been used for Chinese burn practice. But she didn't care. I couldn't remember the last time we'd snuggled. She didn't seem bothered.

Who was this beast? This woman on a mission was not the woman I'd fallen in love with. She was a machine. A sperm collecting machine. And if I didn't give it willingly, I think she would have surgically removed some while I slept.

'I'm a bit tired.' I said one night.

'Haha. Funny.'

'Seriously, I'm knackered.'

'Lie down.'

And that was it. That was the limit to my fight. After she'd had her way with me and told me to clean myself up, I realised something. Women are cruel when they want a baby!

Conversations
with the Wife

'So?' I ask.

Ridiculously long pause.

'Is there anything you want to say?' I continue.

The Wife's looking directly at me. Sort of. She's gone kind of vacant. Like there's something interesting behind me and the only way to see it is to imagine a hole in my head.

'Are you okay, Babe?'

Her left eye twitches.

'You don't have to say it. Your silence is enough.'

I wave her off like I'm not bothered. This is painful to watch.

'You...'

Hang on. Here we go!

'You…'

'Yeeeees?'

'You…'

Come on. Say it!

Her throat ripples with the force of her dry swallowing these hurtful words.

'You were…'

She grasps the door frame for support. I bet her head's spinning.

Just say it.

'You…'

'Say it!'

'Fine, you were right, I said it! You were right. The sofa looks better there.'

'And the table?'

'Yes. That too.'

I stride into the centre of the room with my hands raised to the gods. My imaginary crowd roars in celebration. Single-stemmed flowers and gold coins are thrown at my feet.

'Are you not entertained?'

I drop to my knees and clasp both hands together, shaking them to the sky.

'Mark this glorious day.'

'Calm yourself down,' she says.

The Wife crashes through my victory parade and sits down on the sofa.

Nothing can ruin this occasion. I rise. I am... reborn.

'From this day forth, our relationship will never be the same.'

'If you say so.'

'Finally, we're equals.'

'Sure.'

'No need to thank me.'

'I didn't.'

Her eyes complete a full 360.

'Now go make me a brew,' The Wife commands.

'I don't make the brews around here anymore. My brewing days are over.'

'Really?'

I leave my adoring fans and take a seat next to The Wife on the sofa which is now resting in its optimum position in the corner of the room. By the gods, this is a glorious day.

'You're right again. Your brewing days are over.'

'Thank you for acknowledging that.'

'Change is in the air.'

'Isn't it.'

'Especially since Ove was born.'

'Ay, what? Why?'

'Now you've had the snip, my child-baring days are over. I can put my feet up. Job done. Is sex even necessary anymore? I mean, what's the point?'

'How many biscuits do you want with your cup of tea, Dear?'

A Force of Nature

'Do we really need a doula?' I ask.

'I'm working through a lot of fear. I didn't think I was going to do this again.'

'But a doula? We're doing a full circle and going from the alternative to the mainstream again.'

'Having a doula's not mainstream.'

'Didn't Prince Whatever's wife have one?'

'I don't know. But that wouldn't make it mainstream. That just means she's taking control. Birthing the way she wants.'

'Whatever. What does a doula actually do?'

'Offers support. Helps to organise things on the night. She'll be able to prompt me in ways which we have already discussed. She'll-'

'Why can't I do that? I did it with Arlo.'

'I know, and you still will. It'll just be another birthing companion. She'll be there to support you too.'

'In what way?'

'We'll make plans before the birth. Discuss ways she can support you while you support me.'

'Like what?'

'I don't know. Off the top of my head, she can make us all cheese on toast while we have skin-to-skin with the baby.'

'Oh. Cool.'

'Think of a doula as a close family member. Someone you can trust to look after me but also someone you wouldn't mind asking to put the kettle on too.'

'Right. Sounds good. You got someone in mind I suppose?'

'Yeah. She's only £700 but-'

'£700. Forget it.'

The Wife is skilled at giving me the illusion of choice. She should work in politics. But in fairness, getting a doula was right for us. Where a midwife can offer medical advice, a doula is more about emotional support. Someone able to connect with birth more than I can. I'm the rubbing shoulders, do you want a glass of water? is the baby here yet? kind of birthing partner.

When The Wife went into labour, I was very happy to have the extra support.

It's 11:52 pm. I open my eyes. The Wife is two inches from my face parallel to me in bed. A bit close for comfort, especially since we had garlic bread for tea.

'What's up?'

'I think the baby's coming.'

I can't help but roll my eyeballs dramatically. Don't judge me – she's said this quite a few times recently and it always ends up being a trump.

'I've been awake for an hour. The baby's coming.'

I switch the lamp on and slip into my imaginary doctor's coat. I place a hand on her belly. I touch her head. Her knee.

'What are you doing?'

'Checking you're alright.'

'I haven't fallen off a bike.'

Something is different tonight. Her complexion. The way she's looking at me. During the pregnancy, she's developed a selection of facial expressions that inform me what she's thinking. *Raised eyebrows and stretched cheekbones* mean she's forgotten something downstairs. *I don't need to get it immediately but don't bother getting into bed until I do.* A scrunched-up nose and tight lips clearly mean she's hungry and wants cheese on toast. *I don't need to get it immediately but don't bother getting into bed until I do.*

She looks calm but excited now; aware and determined. Her eyes are sparkly with anticipation. I'm shitting myself. You can do as much prep as you want but when this moment arrives, it's difficult to describe. A mixture of fear and excitement. Like taking ecstasy for the first time or waiting to go on a rollercoaster while watching other people on it screaming in horror.

The key here by the way is preparation. Oh, my days have we prepared the shit out of this. With Arlo, we got stuck into some alternative thinking: Hypno-birthing, home birthing etc. I don't mind sharing this with you, The Wife will probably never read this bit, but I'm totally bored talking about birth, boobs and encapsulating placentas.

I rush downstairs and grab my list off the fridge. I need to calm down. No point in getting stressed out. The first job is to call our One2One midwife. Then fill the birthing pool with warm water. Not above 37.5 ℃. That is circled several times on the list.

Midwife first.

'Hi. It's Adam Glennon. I'm trying to contact our midwife-'

'Emma's not on call tonight. I'm Sarah. I have all your details.'

'What are the chances of that? Never mind. That's fine. We've prepared for this.'

'How's Claire doing?'

'She began experiencing surges about an hour ago.'

'Okay. It will probably be a few hours yet before you need me to come. Keep me updated on her progress and I'll get organised.'

'No worries, speak to you later.'

I run back upstairs, taking two at a time. Calm down, calm down.

'Got a bit of news, Babe. Emma's not on call tonight.'

The Wife's on all fours on the floor.

'That's fine. Did you call Elle?'

The doula!

'Next job on my list.'

'Okay. Is the midwife en route?'

'She said to keep her updated.'

'Call her back. The baby's coming.'

'She said it's unlikely to be within the next few hours.'

'Caaaaalllll heeeer back, nooooow,' The Wife hisses, whispers but also shouts.

I nod and slowly back out of the door.

'Hi, Sarah. The Wife asked me to call you back.'

'Oh. Is it her first baby?'

'No. She's already prowling around the bedroom floor like a lioness.'

'I'll set off now. Should be there within the hour.'

'Great. I'll leave the front door ajar. Just let yourself in.'

Doula next. Then the pool!

'Elle. It's happening.'

'I'll be there in twenty minutes.'

'Amazing.'

Into the lounge to fully inflate the birthing pool which has been sitting in the corner for the last week. For the last baby, I nearly killed myself

blowing it up under pressure. Not this time. I grab the small electric pump from the drawer and attach it to the side of the pool.

One minute later...

Done. Oh yes!

The rest of my list consists of sheets and towel preparation, lights, music, food, and drinks. But filling the pool is next. I catch myself starting to rush again then slow down and walk into the kitchen. I grab everything I need to fill the pool from under the sink. Already tried and tested several times so why oh why does the hosepipe adaptor suddenly not fit on the tap?

Water is pissing out from all angles and it won't fit in the right position.

I turn the water off and try again.

I'm sweating now.

The pool is a fundamental part of the plan. I look down at the adaptor in my hand and give it another go.
Useless.

I stare at it. I will it to fit but as it turns out, you can't weld rubber and metal together with a stern look and hope.

'Babe,' The Wife shouts from upstairs.

'I will never forgive you,' I tell the traitorous adapter.

175

I drop it in the sink and run up the stairs. I smell like a mixture of cabbage and raw meat.

'Little boy.'

Arlo's stood outside the bedroom rubbing his eyes and wearing the floppiest hairdo ever.

'What you doing?'

He points to the bedroom where The Wife is currently making some animalistic noises. I pick up Arlo and turn towards Becca's door just as she appears from her fortress of tech and incense.

'Perfect timing. Can you take him?'

'Come here, little boy,' she says. 'Shall we watch a film on my bed? I've got choccy.'

He pushes me away like an empty plate and they retreat into her room. We want them to join us as soon as the baby arrives so Arlo can see that the new person he's been talking to inside The Wife's belly isn't just the rumbling effects made by wind and packets upon packets of Rich Tea biscuits.

I open our bedroom door and step inside. The atmosphere's thick with energy. Something tangible's filling the room. It's like stepping off a plane on holiday and getting hit by the heat. The Wife's leaning against the wall.

'Are you okay, Babe? What do you need?' I ask.

'Water.'

I pass her a bottle of water. She's very hot. I open a window. It's only been about fifteen minutes since we were lying in bed but she looks like she's been in labour for hours.

'I'll get some fresh water and bring it up. Listen, Babe, the pool isn't gonna happen. The adaptor won't fit-'

'It doesn't matter. There wouldn't be time to fill it anyway. The baby's coming.'

That feels like a twenty-tonne rock's been lifted off my shoulders. I turn and Elle's padding slowly up the stairs with the birthing bag and bottled water. The Wife was right. Having a birthing companion was the right choice for us because watching her walk towards me now with the things I need gives me a warm tingly feeling in my belly.

'Elle. Your timing is, well, perfect.'

She smiles - takes some towels from the bag and places them in front of the armchair. The Wife and Elle whisper to one another then Elle helps The Wife remove her bra from under her t-shirt and holds her steady as she kicks off her pyjama bottoms. They hold hands for a moment then she unscrews the lid from the bottled water, and holds it to The Wife's mouth as she swigs. Then Elle sits in the corner in a meditative position.

This is it. It's time for me to be completely present. I position myself to The Wife's side and begin slowly caressing her shoulders. 'You're doing amazing, Babe. Everything's great. Everything's okay.'

'Is everyone okay?'

'Everyone's fine, Babe. Arlo and Becca are watching a film and eating chocolate.'

'Okay.'

She begins to sway and moan. Unrepeatable swear words are used. She's completely uninhibited. She keeps checking in between her legs as if the baby's head must be hanging out. I'm no expert but I think she's a bit keen there.

She turns towards me. Her eyes are wild. She rags me from side to side by the scruff of the neck with such force I grip the armchair to make sure I'm not thrown across the room.

Her heightened primal strength is so present she could rip the doors off a car. Or even open the Christmas pickle jar which has been sealed in the fires of Mordor!

I relinquish any notion of control.

The Wife is so focused. I think. Or lost. It's difficult to know exactly what she's experiencing. I plant a knee and foot on the floor and grip the armchair. Her arms hang around my neck in a boxer's clinch. Our sweat and heat mix together.

I whisper into her ear, 'I love you. You're amazing.'

There's no sense of time. Nothing else matters. The Wife places a hand between her legs again and again I can't help but think it's too soon. I never really followed all that dilation stuff. But then she releases an ear-piercing scream and splosh... the baby hits the bedroom floor at our feet in a tangle of chord and plasma.

I can't believe it. I put my hands behind my head and look around the room for someone to confirm it's really happened. Elle nods and smiles. The Wife begins to bend for the baby, but I gently hold my arm out, reminding her to take what is known as a "birthing pause." A moment to take in the magnitude of what's been accomplished.

'Babe, you did it. You did it. That was amazing, that was...'

She strokes my face and I kiss her hands. The baby's little cry fills the air.

The Wife collects the baby, still attached to the cord, off the floor and sits in the armchair. Elle wraps a blanket around The Wife's shoulders.

I'm in awe at what I've just witnessed. There's a knock at the bedroom door. The midwife pops her head in and suggests coming back in half an hour to check everything's okay. The door opens a little wider and Becca and Arlo step into the room.

'Is it a girl?' Becca asks.

We had all predicted a girl. The Wife peeps underneath the towel.

'I can't tell.'

'Cake,' Arlo says.

'Come and meet the baby first.'

We all gather around this amazing woman and the smelly bundle of life in her arms.

'Actually, I'd love a piece of cake. And a brew,' The Wife says.

Before I can respond Elle is up and out of the door.

'I'll sort that.'

'Thank you,' I say.

'It smells,' Arlo points out.

'Is it a girl? Becca asks again.

The Wife looks at me.

'Are you ready to know?' she asks.

I already know it's a boy because I'm either looking at some strange growth hanging between his slightly crossed legs or a huge weirdly coloured ball bag.

'Say hello to your little brother, Ove.'

181

For Grape's Sake

I'll be the first to admit my language has been a little blue over the years but having the boys is forcing me to rethink my word choices. It's not often I've let slip anything particularly vulgar but I'm finding it increasingly difficult to keep that adult language under wraps.

Day one: I entered the living room as Ove used porridge to re-decorate a recently painted wall.

'For grape's sake, Ove, sit at the table.'

'No!'

Interfering in his life only motivates him further. He scooped out another handful of porridge from the bowl and turned his attention to the sofa. I considered reaching forward and stopping him but seriously, what's the fu... flipping point?

Day two: I'm juggling bags, coats, and children in my arms. It's raining. One of the kids is kicking off. I drop the car keys on the floor outside the front door.

'Sausages!'

The kids looked at me weird. Even they thought it was pathetic. This charade's not going to last long. I'm not the kind of person who can get away with being nice all the time. But I don't want to swear around the boys. I need to retrain my brain by somehow removing years of council estate conditioning. A lifetime of bad language passed on from one generation to the next.

It began at primary school where I was taught the basics in genitalia-related swear words and accompanying hand signals. The words available evolved during secondary school and into adult life but becoming a dad changed many things and swearing less was one of them. But the urge to swear more often has returned with a vengeance now the boys consistently ignore my pleas for mercy.

Day three: I walked barefoot, what a rookie, out of the kitchen with a boring cup of tea in my hand and stood on the spikiest toy ever created! It stuck horribly into my sole. Shock waves shot through my leg, up my torso, causing my vocal cords to vibrate, releasing words into the world that ideally would have been *for grape's sake* but, unfortunately, were not.

I hobbled over to the armchair and found solace in the fact it wasn't red wine dribbling along my arm onto the carpet. I attempted to gauge what Arlo had heard while furiously rubbing my foot. He didn't seem bothered. Maybe I'd gotten away with that one?

A few hours later: The Wife was on the floor playing with the boys. The trainset had been expertly set up by Arlo but Ove, a destructive force, systematically destroyed all in his path. Before we could intervene, I heard my words repeated back to me.

'For grape's sake.'

(I hope we're all on board here, he didn't say grapes).

The Wife looked at me with one expertly arched eyebrow. I returned that arched eyebrow with an open-mouthed, *oh my goodness, I'm shocked beyond words* kind of expression. I responded with a *where on earth would he pick up language like that? What has the world come to?* Shake of the head and tried to find something else to look at.

I eventually caved in and made eye contact with The Wife again and we engaged in a deep eyebrow-to-eyebrow psychic conversation.

"You knew I was a gobshite when we met," my left eyebrow and slight grin said.

"That's not a very mature defence," her raised eyebrows and twisted lips replied.

"Swearing has nothing to do with maturity," both eyebrows scoffed.

Her nostrils did a little dance, and I knew there was no point arguing about it. Our eyebrows agreed to not draw attention to it any further. Her gently nodding head informed me, *I'm still a good dad but I need to try better next time.*

I agreed with a nod.

Next day: Arlo was doing his thing with the building blocks on a mat when Ove decides to obliterate it all.

'For grape's sake, Ove!' Arlo screamed.

I needed a word. I gently explained to Arlo how Daddy had used a grown-up word the other day and it wasn't bad, just not for children. I suggested using something different. A shift away from grapes or any other food-related replacement.

'How about saying something like, flipping heck?'

We kind of shook on it. All day he muttered "Flipping heck" to himself while playing. Very cute.

That evening: The Wife came home, and we enjoyed an incident-free couple of hours. We were sitting at the table eating tea. All was well. Arlo leaned forward and simultaneously knocked over a glass of water and elbowed his fork, complete with tomato pasta shell, which went flying and splattered onto the floor.

'For grapes heck!' Arlo shouted.

I didn't need to look at The Wife to know her eyebrows were shouting at me again.

Meltdown Timetable

06:30 am

Arlo: 'Morning, Daddy.'

Me: 'Morning, Son.'

Arlo: 'Can I watch a film?'

Me: 'Not first thing, son.'

Meltdown Scale 6/10

06:52 am

Arlo: 'Where's my breakfast?'

Me: 'I'm just sorting it now. Why don't you set the table?'

Arlo: 'I want chocolate.'

Me: 'You know we don't have chocolate first thing.'

Meltdown Scale 7/10

07:01 am

Arlo: 'Where's Daddy gone?'

The Wife: 'He's feeding the cats.'

Arlo: 'Daddy said we could watch a film and have some chocolate.'

The Wife: 'I don't think so, Lovely Boy.'

Meltdown Scale 8/10

7:30 am

Arlo: 'Will somebody play with me?'

Me: 'I'm just tidying the kitchen.'

The Wife: 'I'm going to do some yoga. Why don't we do it together?'

Arlo: 'You're both poo heads.'

Meltdown Scale 7/10

8:00 am

Arlo: 'Can I have a snack?'

Me: 'You've just had breakfast.'

Arlo: 'I'm still hungry.'

Me: 'You're not just stuffing your face all day.'

Meltdown Scale 8/10 - Parent Meltdown 5/10

Arlo: 'Can I have an ice-cream?'

The Wife: 'You've literally got a rice cake in your mouth.'

Arlo: 'But I want an ice-cream.'

The Wife: 'You're not having an ice-cream.'

Parent Meltdown level 6/10

9:28 am

Me: 'Arlo, don't do that to your brother.'

Arlo: 'He likes it.'

Me: 'He's shouting no and trying to run away.'

Arlo: 'He likes it.

Parent Meltdown Level 7/10

9:44 am

Arlo: 'Can we watch the telly now?'

Me: 'We're going for a walk.'

Arlo: 'I want to watch the telly now!'

Me: 'How about this, I take the telly off the wall and smash it to pieces?'

Maximum Combined Meltdown 10/10

9:48 am

Me: 'Yes to everything for the rest of the day.'

Kids: 'Yay!'

A Lockdown Story

'Babe! Babe,' I shout from the bathroom. 'You need to come and see this.'

The Wife comes running towards me with a worried look in her eye.

'What's going on?'

I point down at the washing basket on the floor.

'Look.'

She follows the direction of my finger. I watch her facial expressions change as she moves from annoyed – confused – to enlightened. A look of pure happiness and surprise radiates from every cell in her being.

'It's empty,' she whispers.

'I know.' I place a supportive hand on her shoulder.

'Is this real?' she asks.

We both take a step closer to the empty basket and peek inside. The material is damp. A bit mouldy. It stinks in fact but there it is, the bottom of the washing basket. I don't have to look at The Wife to know her eyes are filled with tears. I'm feeling emotional too.

'But that's not all,' I say.

'Nothing can top that.'

'Follow me.'

I take her hand gently in my own and guide her upstairs past the spikey Lego pieces, over the sticky something and through the pile of soft toys and pillows, to our bedroom. The sunbeams radiate through the window and the clearest blue sky stretches as far as the eye can see. A large metallic clothes maiden is stretched out in front of the window. Sunlight reflects off it and dazzles our eyes. I don't even have to say the words.

'It's empty,' she whispers again.

'There's more.'

The Wife's eyebrows almost leap from her head as she opens her eyes wider than should be possible for a human being. Our hands remain together, tighter, as I pull her from the room back towards the pile of soft toys and pillows. I spot *Marshal* from *Paw Patrol* and kick him in the head, The Wife uppercuts *Peppa Pig* in the face and we blast through the rest, sending them flying through the air.

We enter the kid's bedroom and jump over the piss-stained towel on the floor, over the crusts and half-eaten soggy pear, over the pencil crayons, felt tips, dried out Play-Doh, over one of our paint-smeared naked children, to the window which faces the garden.

'Loooook,' I whisper.

Again, she follows the direction of my pointed finger to the empty washing line hanging lifelessly between the house and the shed. The emotion is too much, and we embrace. We hold each other tight. Our hearts beat in unison. We know this feeling won't last but here and now in this moment, our lives have never been so in-tune. So complete.

We turn on our heels and float out of the room. Nothing can touch us. Our hands stay as one as we glide down the stairs together. Truly together in oneness.

'What time is it?' The Wife asks.

'Nearly lunchtime.'

'Too early for a glass of sparkling?'

'It's lockdown, Babe. It's never too early.'

'I'll grab a bottle from the garage and put it in the fridge.'

'I'll make lunch.'

'Perfect.'

I lean forward, we kiss passionately. It's almost impossible to separate our hands but we manage it. I slide into the kitchen and open the fridge as The Wife heads for the garage.

'What goes best with sparkling wine?'

I empty the shelves of all things cheese and dip related and pile them on the worktop. I grab crisps, fruit, and chocolate! And bread of course. I smile knowing this is going to be a fine feast.

'Daddy,' Arlo enters the room.

'Oh hi, Son. Has the film finished?'

'Not yet. Mummy's crying.'

'Tears of joy, Son.'

'I don't think so. She's on the floor.'

'Ay?'

I leave the feast, pick Arlo up and stride towards the playroom where the internal garage door is. The Wife's curled up on the floor in the doorway. She's not crying any longer, but her eyes are painfully red and her face is whiter than any face I've ever seen. I place Arlo on the sofa.

'Is mummy dying?'

'What? No, Son, just put your film back on.'

He switches the TV back on. I kneel slowly, placing a hand on her cold shaking shoulder.

'Babe. What is it?'

She mutters something.

'I can't hear you.'

She pulls her twitchy hand from her armpit and points into the garage. This time it's my turn to follow the direction of a pointed finger. The garage is gloomy and jam-packed with formless shadows of *stuff*. I don't understand.

'There...' she forces out the word slightly louder than a breath.

My eyes adjust to the light and I see. Now I see. Oh my god, it's enormous. The room begins to spin, and I grab the doorframe just in time before losing my balance. I use it to pull myself into a standing position because if I let myself fall to the floor with The Wife there's a possibility I'll never get up again.

How did I not realise this would happen? How could I be so foolish? Such a rookie. A massive error in judgement. I need to see it properly. I need to face this head-on. I scramble for the switch behind the door and push.

The light pierces my eyes. Blinding me.

I push forward into the room with my hands out in front of me and then stop. There in front of me is the biggest pile of ironing I've ever seen in my life. It appears to be growing up the walls like a hive of fabric. There's a large Ikea shopping bag at the bottom that looks tiny. Ready to burst. It's straining against the sheer magnitude of the weight upon it.

What have I done... what... have I done?

Weekend Breaks

Ha!

Moving House

Moving to a new house is supposed to be one of life's most stressful events. In the top five, some say. Personally, I think that's nonsense. What is stressful is having an overwhelming urge for hangover cheese on toast and mustering the motivation to leave the comfort of your stinky bed, dragging your feet to the kitchen, putting the grill on, making a brew, grating the cheese then opening the cupboard to find that some imbecile has eaten the last of the bread but for some sick – twisted reason has left the plastic bag there with nothing but crumbs inside.

I kid you not, these people exist. You might even live with one of them.

But I suppose stress is subjective, like most things in life. Personally, I love packing. Organising the bejesus out of it. Getting rid of all the bits and pieces scattered or stored around the house which you've been clinging onto for reasons unknown, and finally, have an excuse to sell or donate. It's like some unspoken right of every dad to remove anything he deems not worthy of keeping without discussing it with anyone.

'Have you seen the kid's *Peppa Pig* puzzle?' The Wife asked.

'You mean the one that's been on the kitchen floor for a week?'

'It's not been a week.'

'Trust me, it's a week.'

'Where is it?'

'Gone.'

'Where?'

'You know where.'

'You've sold it?'

'This is a time for honesty, Babe. You're going to find a lot of things have moved on.'

'I knew it.'

'It's better this way. You have complete deniability with the kids.'

'I can't believe this. That wooden toolset?'

'Gone.'

'The plastic sand pit, that coconut instrument, my Spanish ceramic bowl... it's all becoming so clear now.'

'Yes, yes, and yes, Babe. You choose the new house, I decide what goes. It's my rite.'

Kids don't get much of a say in this life-changing event. How do you explain to little ones that you plan on uprooting them from the one place they call home to some strange empty house splattered with dodgy wallpaper and a kitchen with a subtle but noticeable smell of rotten cabbage? There are smells in all the rooms. An emptiness. A sense that other lives have been lived here and now it's your turn to fill that space.

The kids don't understand why this is being thrust upon them. They were happy where they were. That box room which they'll eventually outgrow is theirs. They don't think about size. The scribbles on the walls are theirs. The den under the stairs. The tree out the back. It's the safest place they've ever known.

How do you explain to them that it's a good idea to leave it all behind?

Gently is how. A tip-toe approach is probably best. Or even better, lie to them. Anything to keep the stress levels to a minimum.

When Arlo was three and Ove was a newborn, we got motivated and began the process of looking for a larger house. When you're a social housing tenant you can enter the crazy, and unpredictable world of home swapping. You tidy your house for long enough to put some pictures on a website called Homeswapper.

You have many, many conversations with people who have zero intention of moving but just enjoy playing with your emotions until you finally meet a few like-minded types who appear sane enough to be serious. They come to your house and you pretend your neighbour's not a complete dick and you go to theirs and they pretend no one's ever been stabbed outside the local shop.

You smile and explain how you just never, after three years, got around to painting over that horrendous orange colour in the bathroom and they smile and pretend the holes in the doors are from the kids playing with baseball bats, and we all just smile and bullshit our way to an unspoken agreement, that we know is all lies but you don't mind because you want a dining room, and they want a driveway.

Many obstacles can and do get in the way and people are free to change their minds at the last minute of course. Ha. Ha. Ha. Twice we were left with packed boxes and dismantled furniture after the moves fell through. We didn't achieve the "gently" bit with the kids unfortunately because we got organised far too early.

We were naïve.

We created a confusing atmosphere at home, especially once our possessions appeared back on the shelves. It was probably a mistake to take Arlo to view the potential home swaps because he never misses a trick and listens, even when it appears he isn't, to everything being said. Won't this look good here? The kids will love this room etc etc etc.

 It never occurred to us that it wouldn't happen because we were so determined to move to a new area. We built up the expectation then it crumbled around us, and we didn't know how to reverse all the promises we'd made.

It's difficult to say what Arlo understood, but the uncertainty played out in various behavioural patterns, like suddenly refusing to sleep in his bed because he no longer liked his room. Becoming fearful that ghosts were everywhere, preventing him from enjoying some independent play which he'd always enjoyed. He took a step backwards because there was suddenly an element of uncertainty in his life which hadn't been there before.

And then it happened. From out of nowhere we were contacted by someone who knew everything about our house, road, and neighbourhood, and they wanted it! And they had a large townhouse which they couldn't manage. It felt too good to be true but we were guarded at first.

'I've literally just put new wardrobes in every bedroom. I thought we were staying?'

'Yeah, but... a townhouse?'

'I know, it sounds amazing but I can't be bothered with it all again.'

'Just look at the pictures.'

'I don't want to.'

'It's a townhouse, Babe.'

'I hear you, but...'

'Taaaawwwoooon house!'

'I know...'

'Townhouse.'

'I get...'

'To to to to to tooowon house.'

'Babe?'

'T t t t townhouse!'

'Right, show me the flipping pictures.'

'Yes.'

'Oooo, it has a garage!'

We signed on the dotted line and the process began all over again, but this time boxes were packed and stacked out of sight. We tried to keep the house looking as normal as possible until two days before the physical move when the contracts had been signed and there was no backing out. Then we took Arlo round to see the amazing new house with three floors!

On moving day, I made sure there was lots of cake, nice drinks, Grandparents to play with and a new DVD for him to watch. This held his attention sufficiently while everything happened around him. Ove was a newborn and enjoyed draining every last drop of milk from The Wife so it was difficult for her to multi-task between parenting and organising as I unloaded box after box into each room.

Having a townhouse with three floors is amazing for space.

Having a townhouse with a million stairs... not so amazing for unpacking!

Be Careful

I think I'm turning into a fuddy-duddy. I've started saying phrases like dilly-dallying, dawdle, and fuddy-duddy! What's happening to me? Has a dead nana possessed a part of my brain? Where this leads to worries me more. What's next? Bird watching? Chequered pyjamas? Wearing walking boots everywhere? Even while food shopping!

Shudder.

I want to parent my boys safely, and fairly, but when they mess about crossing the road I should shout, "Get across the road now before you get squashed by that lorry!" I guarantee that would motivate them quicker than dilly dally. Or dawdle. I see other parenting heroes dragging their kids around screaming, "Hurry up ya little shits!" but I'm like, "Hurry up my little chickens, don't dawdle."

Those parents have my respect.

Yeah, those kids might grow up with deep emotional scars, and some addictive tendencies, but at least they won't get run over by a bus or use words like dawdle in public.

But that's just the tip of the iceberg.

My real concern for myself and other parents is the overuse of "Be careful." I found myself telling Arlo, when he was a pre-schooler, to be careful carrying a glass of water. Be careful sitting on the stool. Be careful jumping off the table onto a pile of cushions. I know what the consequences of jumping from the table and missing the cushions are, but I also know how much fun it is when you get it right.

I'm wondering whether there is a better way to communicate my concerns without spoiling the fun?

I began listening out for other parents and how they used it and, oh my, "Be careful" is right up there on a par with "Share." I'll delve into that one another time if I remember. "Be careful," is blurted out repeatably and without any other instructions. The kids don't even know what they're supposed to be careful of.

Children take risks in order to understand the world around them. It's how they understand their limitations. It's their way of exploring their potential. And sometimes they're going to get hurt. And when they do, it's horrible. You want to wrap them up in love and assure them it won't happen again.

Which of course we can't.

It's unrealistic to suggest they'll never climb a tree again or ride a bike after falling. Or if you have kids like mine, simply walking across a room is a potential danger because coordination's the problem. I'm not going to blame the floor and carry them everywhere for the rest of their childhood. Neither would I tell myself I'm never drinking wine again after waking up with zero spit left in my moistureless mouth.

I have a reasonable approach; I don't drink again for at least two days and I pretend all day, to The Wife, that I'm not really dying inside.

Be careful, be careful, be careful!

Is it possible to facilitate risk but minimise the danger? Recently, instead of saying "Be careful" I've highlighted the potential dangers or pitfalls of their decisions in a precise way.

"Son, you do know there's spilt water on the table? Can you see it? You might want to think about where you place your feet before jumping headfirst onto the sofa."

Or.

"Make sure you pick your landing spot before you jump. Have a look around and make sure there's nothing in the way."

Or.

"If you're going to climb over your mum's exhausted body, make sure you use good balancing skills, Son, and try not to step on her boob."

I still want to blurt out "Be careful" at least a hundred times a day because it's so ingrained. But it's definitely fading. And what really matters is the result of making this change. Are the kids hurting themselves less? Are they finding the right balance between safety and adventure?

The simple answer is yes.

But don't take my word for it. See how many times you hear yourself say "Be careful" in a single day. You might be surprised just how annoying you sound.

May the Best
Beast Win

This is rare. The house looks nice. Tidy. It's 10 am and no one's had a meltdown. The boys are playing so calmly together.

'I'm just going to fill the dishwasher, Boys. Back in five.'

'Okay, Dad,' they both reply.

I take a moment to look at them. My heart fills with love. I collect the breakfast bowls off the small table and step into the kitchen.

I'm so blessed

Three, two, one...

Screams fill the air.

I swoop back into the lounge. Both boys are naked and clawing at each other's throats! The chairs are upside down. Every toy shelf has been emptied onto the floor. The sofa cushions are scattered throughout the room.

'What's going on?'

'He, bla, wa, na na, la, la, ra, paaaaa, heeeee!'

I return to the kitchen.

May the best beast win.

Living with Type 1 Diabetes

At the tender age of thirty-three, five months before Arlo was born, I experienced what The Wife describes as a "crisis episode." For two weeks I suffered from the most severe case of dehydration, blurred vision, loss of appetite, weight loss, frequent urination (putting it mildly) and my personal favourite way to go insane, sleep deprivation.

For someone rarely ill, my immediate and unqualified self-diagnosis was I had a bug that would soon be on its way. Or it was brain damage, and this was my new life. And I was going to have to get used to it. Either way, like a typical bloke, I suffered in silence until it became obvious something was wrong.

My symptoms didn't ease - they persisted.

Dehydration: My mouth turned into what can only be described as polystyrene. Liquid would cascade down my chin because it struggled to penetrate the wall of cracked dryness inside my mouth. I would wake in the night short of breath because my inner cheeks and tongue were so swollen and hard that they would clonk together like bricks.

The only mild relief during these sleepless nights was the frozen pineapple chunks I sucked on regularly that managed, for a few blissful moments, to penetrate through the polystyrene - brick dust - excuse for a mouth. Just moistening my insides long enough to trick me into believing I'd gotten over the worse of it.

I basically drank anything and everything I could get my hands on. All day. But it was never enough.

Blurred vision: I've always had excellent eyesight. I have an exceptional left eye apparently. I'm the sort of person who can read a small sign from hundreds of feet away. I've known people (The Wife) to stand in awe at my superhero-like capabilities. But my power had gone. Everything, all the detail and clarity I usually enjoyed was replaced with a haze-like quality. Like having an unwanted switch inside my retinas and turning it to pissed.

I was driving to the seaside, pretending all was well, when the façade was busted.

'We come off at junction nine,' The Wife said.

'Okay, cool.'

Two minutes later...

'You were supposed to come off.'

'Oh. I couldn't see the sign.'

'What do you mean, you couldn't see the sign?'

'Erm, I've got a bit of blurred vision. But I can see all the cars.'

'What? How long have you had blurred vision?'

'I don't know, a week or two.'

'A week... right pull in at the next services. There's one coming up in a minute. Driving when you can't see the sign. Do you know how dangerous that is?'

'We've made it, haven't we? Incident free.'

One minute later...

'You've just driven past the services.'

'How am I supposed to know? I can't see!'

After we swapped drivers and I spilt the beans on the situation, which in truth was a massive relief, The Wife said the words I hadn't even slightly considered.

'Sounds like Type 1 diabetes to me.'

Frequent Urination: Wow, I mean, wow! Has another human being on this planet, ever, I mean ever pissed as much as I did back then? I doubt it. And the smell, wow, oh wow. Four times during the night and hourly during the day. At one point I considered having a catheter inserted to save me the trouble of scheduling my day around having a wee.

Sleep deprivation: A personal favourite of mine. Nothing like a little bit of sleep deprivation to force someone's mind to the edge of insanity. I've always been a light sleeper, surviving on less than most. But there's a breaking point and the worse part of the madness was the nightmares. As mentioned, the dehydration would often keep me awake but once I'd managed to fall asleep, I would dream about water; craving, and searching for droplets of moisture.

I'd wake up panicked, clawing for the pint pot by the side of the bed and drain the contents which would usually just dribble out the sides of my mouth. Then I'd check the time and be deflated to see it was about 1 am which meant I still had the rest of the night to endure.

Only one word sufficiently describes that experience, nothing fancy. . . shit. It was shit!

Loss of appetite and weight loss: I couldn't bring myself to finish a meal. Starting it was hard enough. I love cooking so preparing meals sometimes takes a couple of hours. Not a problem. It's even better with a glass of red. During this time, it was impossible to drink red wine, so in order to build an appetite, I'd have a glass of posh organic beer. The slight fizz and earthy taste was unbelievably refreshing. Then, the anticipation would build, and my mind would communicate with my stomach and they would both agree, that I was indeed starving!

I would smile, present the food to The Wife and Becca, sip my beer, smile a little bit more, and then watch as they tucked in. I'd look down at the plate and all I could see was a pile of dog shit. Appetite gone. Back to square one.

I was desperate to feel normal again.

Once The Wife got involved the GP was contacted and an appointment was made for some blood tests. When the results came back I received a call from the GP's receptionist informing me not to consume any sugar or alcohol over the weekend and that the doctor would see me on Monday morning.

219

I had been drinking sugary everything because that's what I thought I needed. Which was true. Sort of. I was unable to convert the glucose into energy, so my body was using my fat supplies to keep the engine ticking over. I've always had a bit of extra chub around the mid-rift, not enough to feed a group of adults trapped in the wilderness, but definitely enough for a couple of skinny kids!

But it's lucky I had a little extra meat because it meant I had something to keep me going. This may have saved my life.

At this point in my life, I was not fully aware of the effects of carbohydrates and sugar on the blood or how it all worked. What I did know was I already had a low-sugar diet, but like most, I could probably do better. So, plans were cancelled over the weekend and on Monday morning The Wife and I went to the GP to receive the unwelcome news that I had Type 1 diabetes. Life was never going to be the same again.

We sat.

He read from the computer screen.

'You have diabetes.'

The Wife and I nodded our heads and held hands.

'Type 2 diabetes.'

'Erm, what? Type 2?'

He typed out a prescription for Metformin and explained something about diet and British Olympian Steve Redgrave, and off we went to the chemist, too confused to question his opinion.

'It's okay,' I said, 'let's play the game and see how we get on.'

The Wife wasn't convinced.

And she was right.

Let me break down the next month:

- The symptoms worsened.
- I was unable to spend longer than half an hour on my feet.
- Went back to the GP to tell him the Metformin was making me feel sick and it wasn't working. In front of two junior doctors, he said "It will take some adjustment, you'll need to get used to it."
- Secretly believed I was dying.
- Kidney pains started.
- The Wife takes me to Accident & Emergency.

- Almost immediately diagnosed with Type 1 diabetes – Insulin dependent – Type 1 diabetes.

After two nights in the hospital, monitored hourly, given insulin injections and a constant drip filled with saline to stabilise the potassium and ketone levels and bang... I felt normal again. Sort of. Two stone lighter, mentally, physically, and spiritually battered but definitely more normal.

Were we angry at the GP? The Wife was. I was relieved more than anything. That month had been a living nightmare and I was just happy to be able to sleep at night without the horrible dreams or getting up dozens of times for a wee. Once we knew it was Type 1 Diabetes, I was able to move forward and take a bit of control back from the illness.

The GP had been right about the adjustment period though; figuring out the right amount of insulin to take with meals is like a game. The shittest game I've ever had the misfortune to play. Hypoglycemia, that's low blood sugar, is a very real danger. It's a massive pain to manage, no doubt about it. When I see people munching on a piece of cake, or even just a sandwich, I think to myself, you lucky bastard. After a while, I got tired of checking my blood sugar levels all the time. Thinking about it. Worrying about it.

It's not fun.

So, I got experimental and altered my diet. I tried gluten-free, plant-based, paleo and several more. Most diets led back to the same place; diabetes burnout. This is when you get exhausted from thinking about it. And usually leads to binging on pizza, chocolate and all the other things that make eating fun but managing blood sugar levels difficult.

Completely cutting foods from my diet was clearly not the way to go long term.

It's taken a few years but I've achieved some balance. I keep complex carbohydrates down to a minimum. Intermittent fasting is amazing and I only eat snacks when drinking alcohol. I've got used to having salad with curry, spinach instead of pasta and several other variations. Most important of all is being able to parent my boys without the threat of hypoglycemia.

High blood sugar (hyperglycaemia) on the other hand, causes a lack of empathy and grumpiness, which is also something I keep an eye on as well. But occasionally, on absolute rare occasions, The Wife might suggest I need to check my blood because I'm being a bit snappy. So I do, and I can confirm with all certainty and truth, that each and every single time I'm grumpy, moody, irritable or mean, is because I have high blood sugar. 100% certainty.

Conversations
with a Teenager

I push the creaky bathroom door open.

There are no tubs of cocoa-based products cluttering the window - blocking all-natural light from passing through the glass. In fact, the shelf is clean. The bathroom's clean.

Too clean. Something's not right.

I head to the kitchen with anticipation building in my stomach.

Could this be the day?

I open the cabinet door.

It's full. Over-filled. My heart thuds against my chest as I reach for the dishwasher. It's empty. I'm... confused. This has never happened before.

Becca has brought all the glasses and cups down from her fortress of technology and placed them in the dishwasher. And not only that, she's turned it on, waited for it to finish then emptied it.

And that's on top of cleaning the bathroom.

Watery stuff fills my eyes. Maybe this is the beginning?

I'm so happy.

I win this round.

That's 5432 to Becca and 1 to me.

It's a start.

A Lockdown Story

The second lockdown is not going to be like the last one. Many lessons have been learnt but it'll be different, mainly, because we're moving to Devon. Goodbye Stockport. *We've been together for nearly forty years but it's time we started seeing other towns. It's not you, it's me. Well, it's kind of you, but this is healthy. Amicable. You'll find someone who truly appreciates you I'm sure.*

We can thank the lockdowns for this change. It helped The Wife and I reevaluate. We had the time and space to work through several issues and come out the other side feeling fresh. We had a plan. It wasn't plain sailing though. Things had to get a bit messy before they got better.

From the end of March 2020 to the beginning of June 2020, we were stuck in a cycle. Asking the same questions each day: "What day is it?" "How many snacks do you think we've had?" "When was the last time I showered?"

It became a habit to open wine with lunch.

"Well, it's 7 pm somewhere, hahahahah."

And there was the boredom to contend with.

Wandering around the same streets over and over again, searching for some secret space, a strange tree, an unknown park, anything to break the monotony of lockdown. Anything that offered sanctuary from the mental and physical strain of lockdown with small children. For an hour. Five minutes. Any amount of time! Just a moment to watch my boys play independently without them asking me questions about the complexities of the human psyche, or about *Peppa Pig's* continual promotion of gender stereotypes.

Or more relaxed topics like what is electricity made of?

Or why does poo stink?

Usually, I'm more than happy to answer any questions the boys throw at me. I love playing and I absolutely know the importance and benefits of the great outdoors but halfway through the first lockdown in 2020, I just couldn't be bothered anymore.

'We need to get them out for a bit,' The Wife nudged me between the ribs.

'I don't want to do anything.' I felt nothing. 'I'm too bored to move.'

'There's a post on Facebook about some fairy doors that have been put up around the streets,' she informed me.

'You're trying to tempt me off the sofa with fairy doors? Ha.'

'The boys neeeeed to get out, they're doing my head in.'

I scraped my chin against the shards of delicious sea-salted crisps sprinkled around my chest and neck, away from the Buy 12 bottles of wine, delivered to your house within the hour advertisement on my phone, towards The Wife's bloodshot teary eyes that were staring into my soul - pleading with me to do something with the boys.

'What time is it?'

'The clock is right there,' she pointed with her annoyed head.

'Hmmpff.'

I scraped my chin back the other way towards the silver clock hanging on the wall that was tick-tocking away. I'd never noticed before, but it was suddenly the loudest clock I'd ever heard. So ridiculously loud that it hurt my ears.

How had I never noticed before?

God, I was so bored. I just needed to get up and go look at the damn fairy doors!

A burst of energy surged into my legs and arms, sent from a part of my brain which wants to support The Wife and recognises her cry for help. I saw the solution clearly in my mind's eye but, as quickly as it came, it went.

'It's half eleven,' I told her.

'So?'

'It's lunchtime.'

'It won't hurt you all to miss a meal.'

'I'm not going to rise to that comment.'

I zoned out again and continued with a very important task which was happening beneath my grubby t-shirt then removed my hand to reveal a greyish, bluey, brownish piece of belly button fluff wrapped in black hairs which I held high in the air.

'Look at the size of that,' I marvelled.

The Wife pressed a hand to her throat.

'You're disgusting. What's wrong with you?'

I held it higher.

'This is a record breaker.'

Higher!

'Have you ever seen a piece of belly button fluff as big as that?'

'You need help.'

'This should be named after me, like a new star. Or put in a London museum next to that blob of fat they found in the sewer.'

For reasons beyond my knowledge, she didn't share my enthusiasm. Each quarter of her face seemed to point in different directions and twitched simultaneously. I was afraid.

'Did someone say, fairy doors? What a great idea. Come on kids!'

The Cycle of No

It took a while before it became a conscious thing for me. This cycle of no. I'd observed The Wife doing it for years with a lot of success. No matter how much they screamed or cried, she never caved. It was a sight to behold.

Completely stone cold.

I felt it was a bit dictatory if I'm honest, but she lets me go to the pub and occasionally play with her boobs, so I've never questioned this totalitarian regime.

'Mum, can I have a snack?'

'No.'

'Mum, can we watch a film?'

'No.'

'Mum, can I have a drink of water.'

'No.'

'Mum, have you got a plaster?'

'No.'

She made it look so easy. The pure no-ness of it all. How did she do it so devoid of emotion? So detached? It was amazing. I'm not cut from the same cloth, you see. I'm still wearing L plates whereas she's been a mum for about fifteen years longer than me. Many of the parenting pitfalls I come across she's already navigated. Oh, and how she likes to let me know that at every opportunity.

'I'm going to let them stay up late and watch another film,' I said. Bursting with enthusiasm.

'Hmm mm.'

'What?'

'Nothing.'

'I know that face.'

'What face?'

'That face.'

'I don't know what to tell you.'

Pause for effect...

'But if you let them stay up late it'll be a nightmare getting them to sleep. They'll be overtired and full of sugar. They'll turn nasty and it'll end in tears,' she tells me.

'How can they turn nasty watching *Toy Story*?'

'Hmm mm.'

'I'll deal with them.'

'I know you will.'

An hour later...

'Say it,' she says.

'No.'

'Say... it.'

'You were right okay. You were right. They're horrible ungrateful beasts.'

I'm soft. I see that. I have faith that everything will be okay in the end if you just give them what they want. Or at least make a deal. I know it's ridiculous, but I think I know why. I got a lot of nos as a child.

There was no negotiation. You had the right to storm off in a mood but there was no point arguing about it. I want the scales to tip more to the yes rather than no. Mainly because I want an easy life but also because the things they ask for, overall, aren't unreasonable.

'Dad, can we go to the park?'

'Yes.'

'Dad, can we play little dragons?'

'Yes.'

'Dad, has mum always been your boss?'

'Yes – no. We're a team, Son.'

'Ha ha. Whatever.'

I've been a stay-at-home parent a few times while The Wife has pursued her career interests, so I've had to develop some parenting techniques that don't involve using a super deep authoritarian voice or putting a symbolic foot down! I'm all about physical play. Dens, sword fighting, wrestling, repetitive games of hide and seek over and over again. Anything to keep them from realising I'm just filling time before mum returns and I can do nothing!

I like a smooth ride.

'Dad, can we have a snack?'

'It's nearly lunchtime, can't you wait?'

'No.'

'Okay, I tried. Here you go, lovely boy.'

Good old-fashioned misdirection worked for ages when they were toddlers. They asked for a snack, I showed them a balloon, and they forget what they'd asked for. Bubbles were very effective. *Lion King* was an absolute winner. But techniques like that only lasted so long.

Eventually, you need to bend down to spitting level and try and reason with the little beasts. Of course, they can't have everything they want but my boys are skilled at convincing me I'm wrong. That I'm the one being unfair.

They are relentless in the pursuit of the things they want. When they've had cereal, fruit, toast, crackers, more fruit, water, juice, an ice lolly, a cheese sandwich with cucumber and crisps, more fruit and it's not even lunchtime, I start to question my sanity. How can they have all that and then scream and shout over a rubbish milk biscuit that tastes like sand?

It makes no sense to me. What am I supposed to think? That they would cause such a fuss because of some need for autonomy over their own lives or something?

Crazy teacher talk!

That was the old me. I beat *him* to a bloody pulp and placed him in a large box in my subconscious with the guy that thinks you must iron both sides of a t-shirt. I know how to access the cycle of no now.

One day it just happened. Something snapped.

'Dad, can we watch another film?'

'Ye... no.'

Both boys stopped chewing and looked up from their feeding buckets.

'What was that?' Arlo said

'Ahem... I said no.'

Ove kicked his small wooden table to one side. His feeding bucket and organic bamboo cup hit the laminate floor and he leaned forward off his chair. He was just about to lift his food-splattered naked body up, with the intention of kicking off big time, when Arlo placed a loving hand onto his heaving chest.

Arlo never took his eyes from the organic bamboo cup of juice raised two inches away from his mouth.

Cool as fuck.

'I got this,' Arlo told his brother.

He took a sip from the cup then passed it to Ove who finished it in one, wiped his mouth with the back of his hand then threw the cup over his shoulder, adding it to the rest of the mess on the floor. Arlo patted Ove's chest once more.

Arlo looked at me for the first time since I dared to utter that forsaken word.

'See that mess there?' Arlo pointed with his chubby thumb. 'That's nothing.'

'I'm well aware of your capabilities, Son.'

'So why do it to yourself, DAD?'

'Dad now is it? What happened to Daddy?'

He removed the dented top hat he'd been wearing since dawn and threw it across the room. Just missing my head. He brushed the crumbs and unidentified sticky objects off his underpants then licked his finger – grimaced slightly then did it again. He walked towards me with the physicality of a boss having to deal with the incompetence of his staff for the hundredth time that day.

'I'm guessing, because we've watched three films already, you think it's about time we turn it off. Maybe do some colouring? A bit of home learning? Let me guess, you want to do some baking?'

I looked through the doorway into the kitchen where I'd already organised the ingredients for carrot and walnut muffins.

'I bet you've already separated the ingredients into bowls,' Arlo said.

He looked sickened by the predictability of it all.

'I... er.'

'Let me tell you how this is gonna go.'

Arlo stepped towards me pointing at the doorway to the kitchen.

'You're going to go in there and bake those muffins. If mum asks later, I'll say we all did it together, if that makes things easier on you. You'll say we can only have one muffin' but we'll have at least three.'

He smirked and clapped his hands together real slow and deliberate.

'Mum will be like, "You're such a good Daddy," and we'll be like, "He's the best." Then mum will say, "Why don't you have a glass of wine? I'll put the kids to bed." Doesn't that sound perfect?'

'You think you know me so well,' I tell him.

'You never know, she might even say, "Why don't you go to the pub for a few beers, Babe?" Doesn't that sound even better?'

'I've thought of an alternative actually.'

'You have?'

He used the end of a toy dragon to pick food from in between his teeth. He inspected a scrap of flesh on the dragon's tail then put it into his mouth and swallowed. He nodded his head, ready to negotiate. The dragon flew across the room and landed in a basket below the window near where I stood.

'Go on,' Arlo said.

'Picture this scene,' I said stepping towards him. 'Mum comes home, and the place is a wreck. I'm a wreck. Close to tears. "The boys have been awful, Babe. I don't know what's wrong with them," I'll say. She'll hug me tight. Kiss my cheek. "I didn't have time to clean up or make any tea, Babe. I'm sorry. They've just been so uncontrollable," I'll tell her.'

'You wouldn't do that?'

'I wouldn't do that you say. You know how much mum looks forward to one of my nice teas after a busy day don't you?'

'She loves it.'

'How about this, "I can't cope, Babe. Maybe I should get a full-time job and we'll pay for childcare? Or maybe you should go part-time and you have them?"'

'You couldn't handle a full-time job anymore.'

'Couldn't I?'

We stared into each other's souls.

'You won't pay for other people to bring up your kids.'

'Wouldn't I?'

I had him on the ropes and he knew it.

'One more film then we'll...'

'NO!'

That time I said it so clearly. With confidence. It was biblical. Ove fell back off his chair and thrashed and wriggled on the floor like he was searching for a hot piece of coal on his skin. Arlo stumbled back to the sofa, weak at the knees, weak in the gut!

'We're going to clean up this mess. Turn the telly off. Bake the muffins and then go for a walk. Okay?'

They didn't answer.

They didn't need to.

I had experienced a parenting revolution. I had entered into... the cycle of no!

Baby Wearing's Cool

'Here we go again,' I said.

'Trust me, all the cool dads wear them,' The Wife tells me.

'Where? Who?'

'Chorlton dads.'

'We don't live in Chorlton.'

'You could bring the cool to Stockport?'

'You do realise, only a massive nerd would ever say something like that?'

The Wife has a habit of trying to lure me into doing something a little alternative by placing the word cool somewhere in the conversation. I don't know why she bothers. I already know I am. How? I smoke roll-ups with liquorice Rizla when drinking wine. I wear a flat cap. I don't watch football and I do the ironing!

That's pretty cool, right?

'Will you try?' She continued.

I looked down at the multicoloured stretchy thing in her hand. This was going to be a defining moment in my life as a dad. A line in the sand. Once stepped over there was going to be no way back. The Wife was going to start talking to me about this stuff all the time. Try to include me. Make me go places and talk to people I have zero interest in.

But this meant a lot to her. I could tell by the way she looked at me with this don't you want to have a shared interest bollocks.

'Sure, why not?'

'Yay.'

In case you have no idea what a stretchy is, I'm talking about slings. Carriers. Babywearing. And if you have considered giving it a go, but for whatever reason, you're resistant, which I totally get because if like me you thought you'd look like an idiot, I'm just going to admit it right now, it's great.

I love it!

Not a big fan of talking about it excessively like The Wife and her slingy mums do. It's verging on a cult if I'm truthful. They gather in large groups inside musty-smelling church halls and fill tables with every type of baby-wearing paraphernalia in existence.

The vicars stay well out of the way as these women, drenched in hormones and lavender, sway to some distant drum beat from one side of the room to another with their babies, or toddlers, latched onto their milky boobs.

They advise and congratulate each other on the suitability of their chosen sling or carrier while reminding each other how the slings won't depreciate in value. It's safer than investing in gold I overheard one of them say while munching on a mound of chocolate cake and tandem-wearing her ginormous twins.

As a baby-wearing dad, I'm fussed over something crazy when I arrive. And I love it. Crafty hands all over the place. Pulling, grabbing, and flattening parts of my body ensuring Arlo is secure.

The Wife has no problem with it because it's all in the name of babywearing.

But having a cool dad on board is not the top prize of the day oh no. I'm pushed to the side like a half-chewed chicken leg when a fresh-faced new mum barges in through the heavy double doors with a high-tech John Lewis pushchair worth more than my car.

The slingy mums release a collective sigh, forget whoever, or whatever they are doing, and head straight towards the new mum. All comradery's out the window as they push and hustle for position to see who is going to match this newbie with the right baby-wearing solution.

The new mum doesn't stand a chance.

In a whirlwind of colour and cake, she's quietly separated from her brand-new pushchair which gets parked in the far corner of the hall with the rest. Dusty relics destined to rest amongst their own kind until the end of time. Sad and yet beautiful like a great elephant graveyard. Sacred and not to be disturbed.

The new mum might leave one high-tech pushchair short but her initiation into the cult of baby-wearing is complete once her crying baby settles inside the woven sling expertly wrapped by several of her new kin.

'My baby's stopped crying,' Newbie says.

'Hmm mm,' her new sister's reply.

'But she never stops.'

'Hmm mm. You're one of us now.'

I love wearing Arlo. We look damn cute together. And we certainly don't get bored of all the attention we get while out and about. I had no idea of the pulling power of having a kid. Pulling power might be laying it on a bit thick. It's mainly nanas and grannies stopping us but we love it anyway!

'Isn't he gorgeous,' random granny says.

'Don't call me that, he gets jealous,' I reply.

Wink, wink, nudge, nudge. How we laugh!

Besides all that, baby-wearing is about closeness. Bonding with your baby. I quickly moved away from stretchy woven slings and found a carrier with buckles on the straps which were easy for me to handle. Slings were designed for people with a dexterity beyond my skill level.

Useful points to consider if you're not sure:

- You can carry your partner's shopping bags around town.
- Your hands are free so you can make breakfast, dinner, and tea. wash the pots, hoover, and generally tidy the house, while mum eats cake.
- Babies love it in the sling. It calms them down when they're having a meltdown or need sleep.
- You can make the cake while your partner tells you about a sling that she wants.
- You and the baby feel closer.

If you'd told me a few years ago I'd be talking about baby-wearing, in any way shape or form, I would have said you were high. The truth is, I felt like a bit of a spare part when Arlo was born. The Wife was his everything and my role was more about supporting her. Which, of course, is fine but it was difficult to know my place as far as the baby was concerned.

He wasn't really soothed by my touch and I couldn't feed him because my stupid nipples didn't do anything! Baby-wearing helped me feel closer to him while not really needing to try very hard. I'm not suggesting baby-wearing's the best or only way to go.

It worked for me and any future dads able to try it out should give it a go. What's the worst that could happen? Getting a bit of attention from a silver lady? You can handle it.

Conversations
With the Wife

'Don't say it.' I say.

'Don't be like that.'

'I've just painted the bannister.'

'We've got new flooring too.'

'I'd forgotten about that.'

She pours me a glass of red and passes it to me.

'It doesn't matter about those things.'

'Easy for you to say, I do the work.'

'You like doing it though.'

'I do have other interests you know?'

'Like what?'

'I was thinking of doing a night course.'

'In what?'

'Erm... horticulture.'

'Rubbish.'

I sip my delicious wine. She's got this all planned to a T.

'The thought of dismantling the wardrobes. Boxing everything up.'

'What about it?'

'Classic you. You only see the results, not the work that needs doing.'

'I just get in the way. Better to just leave you to it.'

She empties my favourite lightly sea-salted crisps into a bowl. I take one. Tasty!

'It's not a problem, to be honest.'

'Sorted then. I'll let them know.'

'Hang on. Don't you think we need to talk about a few other issues first?'

'Like what?'

'Like what? ... like moving to the other end of the country and house swapping with strangers.'

'We've done it before.'

'Not to the other end of the country we haven't.'

'And with no support.'

'You're not selling this.'

'We don't have much support now.'

I sip my wine and munch my crisps.

'Plymouth is near Cornwall, yeah?'

'Next door.'

'I've always wanted to go down there.'

'Exactly.'

'Can we really be bothered moving the boys again?'

'I didn't say it would be straightforward.'

'Do they have any Beach Schools?'

'All sorts.'

'Near the house?'

'Uh huh.'

She sips her wine and nibbles a large crisp.

'How far from the house?'

'Not that far.'

'How far?'

'About half an hour.'

'On foot?'

'In the car.'

'Too far.'

'It might be a quick half an hour.'

'Ha ha. You really believe that don't you?'

'They don't have to go every day. '

'That's true.'

'We don't need to work every day either.'

'I like that.'

'The rent is half.'

'Now I'm listening.'

'So that's settled.'

'Chill.'

I switch the telly on and sit back.

'I'm not rushing into a decision.'

'We need to decide ASAP.'

'Why?'

'There's a deadline for the other family to get their kids into grammar school.'

'Did they tell you that?'

'Yep.'

'So, they're serious then?'

'Very.'

'Can we be bothered?'

'It'll be like living on holiday.'

'Now you're talking.'

'Beach every week.'

'Every week?'

'Every day?'

'We could get a dog?'

I knew there was more to this.

'No way.'

'Why?'

'Honestly?'

'Yeah, why?'

'I can't be bothered picking the shit up.'

'Arrr.'

'I see people picking shit up and I just think, nah, you're a slave.'

'I agree. No dog.'

'Defo need wetsuits though. Fancy a bit of wild swimming.'

'We could get a boat?'

'Like a canoe?'

'A sailboat.'

'Piss off.'

Talking to Strangers

There are many sayings from childhood that spring to mind now I'm a parent.

"Wash behind your ears or spuds will grow there."

Classic.

"Don't pick your nose - your head will cave in."

Used by every primary school teacher throughout the 1980s.

I guess they're supposed to be fun, yet I can't help but think that at the core they instil a sense of fear within a child's easily coerced mind. You know, back in the good old days when children were to be "seen and not heard," and it was the norm to give your kids a good smack now and again. For their own good, of course.

Knowing Arlo as I do, he thinks very literally and if I said his head will cave in if he picks his nose, I reckon he'll be discussing it in therapy for most of his adult life.

What we want is for children, anyone really, to not pick their noses while having a civil conversation with them.

'Can you stop doing that while we're talking please?'

'Wait a second, neeearly got it.'

Once the rooting is complete, the picker is faced with that universal decision; whether to wipe it on the furniture or roll it into a ball and flick it across the room. Or, option three, a popular choice with kids, eat it! I've witnessed a few bloody noses as a result of over-enthusiastic rooting - suffered a few myself and I've seen some humongous bogeys balanced on the end of proud fingers. But I have never, not once, seen or heard of a child's head imploding while doing it.
'Good morning, children,' The headteacher says.

'Gooood mooooorning, Miss.'

'I have some terrible news. We've been informed that Steven Parkes from year 4, who was caught picking his nose yesterday while queuing for lunch later suffered from a collapsed head. His parents said he's now three inches smaller. Let this be a lesson to you all!'

Never happened.

And spuds behind the ear! Don't get me started. I remember checking while in the bath, convinced I must have some. It's hard to connect with the distant memory but the residue of confusion was very clear. The last thing I would have thought of doing back then was ask someone if it was true or not. Oh no. Much better to allow the thoughts to rattle around inside my brain unchallenged and able to mutate into something much worse.

I don't want my boys to be confused about their bodies.

I remember lying on my Nana's sheepskin rug when I was about eight, and from nowhere I was struck suddenly by one of those uncontrollable shivers that move through your whole body. I'm eight, so I don't give it much thought. You just accept it as another one of those weird body things no one talks about; like constipation and that crusty bit in your eye unhelpfully referred to as "sleep."

I shivered. I accepted. I moved on.

But then my Nana said, 'that's someone walking over your grave.'

Mind blown!

I was watching *H.R. Pufnstuf* on VHS at the time, which was mental enough, but this was next level. I don't think a week passes without reliving that moment and linking it to my childhood curiosity about the supernatural and all things weird. Was someone walking over my grave in the past or the future? Was my Nana a time traveller? Why was someone walking over my grave anyway? Have they no respect for the dead?

My life was never the same.

Some sayings were quite sensible though. More like instructions.

"Stop, look, listen and think."

A lifesaving instruction that was drilled into us and for good reason. But I think there's one saying which trumps them all. It was blasted into my impressionable young mind from all directions by family members and teachers alike:

"Don't talk to strangers."

Right. I get it. I understand why this was promoted so fiercely. The world can be harsh. Dangerous. We know there are people out there capable of hurting children. History shows us what they are capable of.

The horrific Moors murders of the 1960s were probably still fresh in the minds of the adults of the 1980s, which meant they were very aware of the potential dangers out there. Then in 1990 two boys abducted a toddler and the world was faced with some scary truths; suddenly, children weren't even safe from their own.

Strangers weren't just men and women trying to entice little ones into cars with sweets anymore. Danger was everywhere.

Don't talk to strangers had never been more vital.

Scary times.

But, for me and my boys in the here and now, our days are significantly brightened by our interactions with strangers. I talk to strangers every day. Random grandad outside the supermarket. A nana on the bus. Other parents at the park or library. My boys see this and know that it's natural to interact with others.

When we enter Stockport library, I let my boys explore. I allow a little feral. Controlled feral. Not pushing all the books off the shelves feral. There are spinning chairs in the middle of the main area and they're lots of fun to sit on and use for imaginative play. The bookcases are perfect for playing hide and seek and chase. You're probably reading this and thinking it doesn't sound like suitable behaviour for a library... and you're absolutely right. Will not argue with you on that one.

Most of the people there tap away on keyboards, read books, and generally just ignore my kids or others with similar feral plans. Sometimes parents, like me, who are trying to offer their children freedom while respecting the right of other users to not be dribbled on or disturbed, will gravitate towards each other, discuss their feral kids, and play the who's-had-less-sleep game. I always win.

There are so many social issues to consider while interacting with new people. I have an appreciation for a person's personal space and their right to be left alone. There are social anxieties, cultural differences and a vast array of other reasons why a stranger may not want to interact with you or your touchy-feely kids. I explain to both boys the importance of understanding personal boundaries and how to judge through people's facial expressions and body language whether they want to interact or not. They don't always get it right but I try and stay alert to their movements so I can jump in before Ove climbs up on some random guy's knee and starts rewording his emails on the library computer!

But how can they learn to relate to strangers and navigate tricky social interactions without the opportunity to practice and engage? They can't, can they? There's risk involved of course. Allowing them to push the boundaries may result in them receiving a telling-off from someone.

The interaction would then present an opportunity to explain to the boys what had happened, how it had escalated, and how it could be avoided in the future. And I'm sure they'd nod, pretend to understand, and then do it again five minutes later.

We want to keep our children safe. But in the same breath, we don't hide all the knives in the kitchen or put armbands on them each time we visit a park to feed the ducks. A spot of common sense is required me thinks. Instead of saying don't talk to strangers, we tell our boys to never go **anywhere** with **anyone** without letting us know first. We've told Arlo, as gently as possible that not everyone you meet is a good person.

We've discussed characters in films who enjoy hurting children or animals (Cruella De Vil is a good example) and this helped to give a little context to the conversation.

There is a saying that sprung to mind recently. Something I have extensive knowledge of. Ever heard the one about playing with your willy too much? That it'll drop off! Guess what? Mine's still fully attached, and I've been playing with it for years. I am genuinely concerned for Arlo's well-being though. If he continues tugging on his, with an enthusiasm I've never witnessed before, he could be the first to lose it.

'Dad. It came off.'

'I didn't think it was possible, Son. But you proved me wrong.'

'What am I going to do now?'

'You're going to stop picking your nose for a start.'

Car

I'm fucking disgusting. Rotting pieces of food are stuck to parts of my interior that are growing an ecosystem. I'm pretty sure there's enough penicillin developing on strange furry things to heal gangrene! And the crumbs!

There's not a crease or fold in a seat that is not drowning in the stuff. Ever heard that saying about there being more stars in the sky than grains of sand on all of the beaches? That's fuck all compared to the crumbs in me.

"I'll clean it at least once a month," He said when we drove out of the garage. Yeah, what a load of shit. I was happy then. My previous owner was old and considerate. Had one of those mini hoovers and everything. I used to smell of pine trees and lemon cleaning spray. Smells that just blended nicely together.
Now I'm it's just wet dog and black banana skins - and they don't even have a dog for-fuck's-sake. Although according to Her that's the next thing on her list.

Great.

Talking of her - she takes the piss. If you've ever seen her out and about you'd think, there's a tidy woman. Clean looking - minty fresh. It's a facade! Nonsense. She'll pile apple cores and wrappers in the door pocket until it's almost impossible to close the fucking door. Then when the wind whips some of the wrappers into the street she's always like, "Oh my, how did that happen?"

Facade!

And those kids!

I know it's not cool to say horrible things about little ones but they're on a whole other level. They don't give a shit. Not one tiny shit. They're truly the most disgusting creatures imaginable.

If it's not food or dribble getting wiped all over me it's snot. The older one will dig into his nostrils and gouge huge greeny-brown lumps of snot out - marvel at it for a moment then smear it, slowly, over the back of my passenger seats.
I'm pretty sure he's trying to create a piece of art because it definitely resembles something that belongs in a gallery!

The little one has got some serious coordination issues. He cannot simply put food directly into his mouth. I don't think he's ever eaten a full bag of crisps in one go. Most of it ends up encrusted in my mats on the floor! And when this kid eats an ice cream... I mean, there just aren't the correct words to describe this disaster. No wonder he's always hungry and asking for more.

266

His first word was "snack" for-fuck's-sake!

Oh, and that teenager of theirs who appears out of the blue now and again. Her farts are so powerful - so rancid, I'm stained with the stench of it. The smell has seeped into every fibre of my being and become a part of me. Which I think you'll agree is fucking bang out of order!

But what can I do? Nothing. All I can do is hope He impregnates Her with another one of these disgusting creatures so they'll need a bigger car. That would be amazing. I can see it now. They would have to give me a proper cleaning - probably have to pay for it to be done by a professional. Then a kind-looking elderly gentleman will appear and see me for who I really am. He'll see the telltale signs of misuse and he'll take me away from these ungrateful savages. And together we'll drive off into the sunset while listening to *Smooth FM* and never again will I be subjected to this level of abuse.

Fuck Off, Glue Ear

There's no doubt about it, I suspected life would change significantly when I became a parent. The Wife had gently, over several months, informed me that I'd have to alter some of my personal habits, rituals or quirks, as I like to call them.

- Stop drinking alcohol every night – Tick. No problem.
- No recreational drugs (on weeknights) – Pfff, done!
- The house can't be tidy all the time – We'll see about that Mrs.
- Control my youthful urges – Erm... why?

I'm a smart man - got me a degree and everything - so I also knew there'd be some additions to my already jam-packed modern man chores.

- Learn a million new skills I was not previously equipped to manage – Ongoing.
- Be more sensitive, learn to cry again, explore and share my feelings – Smashed it!
- Put the baby to bed – Erm... Nope.

Why? Our babies have no interest, whatsoever, in being put to bed by me or anyone else except The Wife. And even then, it's tricky. It all started with Arlo. If The Wife had the audacity to peel herself away from him when he was a baby, maybe to get a drink, maybe to treat herself to a nice long wee that wasn't cut off mid-stream, he would sense the milky nipple had been removed from his immediate vicinity and wake up screaming. If she even thought about sneaking downstairs to devour a packet of biscuits, no way mama! He would scream the house down.

She might have reached the bedroom door, slid her dressing gown off the hook, and eased it slowly onto her tired shoulders - feeling confident, or naïve, she may have taken one final look behind her, just to check if he was asleep, and he'd be sat up straight, questioning with his watery eyes, "Where the hell do you fink you're going with my supper? Get back to bed now!"

We were completely at a loss for what to do. Not aided by unhelpful suggestions to leave him to scream it out of his system, or doctors who said he'd grow out of it. It was a lonely place to be. Was it night terrors? Past life regression? We tried Reiki, and a Cranial Osteopath. We went gluten-free goddamnit!

We hired the Native American guy from the *Poltergeist* film to check if the house was buried on an ancient burial ground, but even he'd never seen a child scream so violently, and with so much dribble. He just threw the burning sage onto the floor and jumped headfirst through the bedroom window, never to be seen again.

Nothing worked.

Sleep deprivation causes many things. None of them is fun. Anxiety. Mood swings. Lack of empathy... and, erm... probably something to do with short-term memory loss but I forgot! Have you ever experienced a comedown from amphetamine? It was like that but without the good bit first where you clean the house and feel thin.

We began anticipating the screams. Our rigid bodies filled with anxiety because being woken from REM sleep to the horror of our reality every fifty minutes was worse than pre-empting it and trying to soothe him before it escalated. Which, of course, meant never sleeping.

After two and a half years, The Wife read an article online about children misdiagnosed with ADHD when in fact they were suffering from glue ear: Delayed speech, mouth breathers, unbelievable amounts of dribble and mood swings. The list went on and Arlo hit every point on it. This knowledge was the catalyst for change.

We had to harass our GP for a referral to the ENT department. Pumping him full of painkillers helped but having grommets in both ears and the adenoid removed was the real game changer.

Life got significantly better for all of us after that. Not perfect by any means but we started to get at least four hours of sleep on the bounce and that was flipping amazing.

Then Ove began exhibiting all the same symptoms as Arlo had. We couldn't believe it. At this point I won't lie, I felt sorry for us the parents, not the kids. But at least we knew what to look out for, so we were right on it! We weren't going to take no for an answer from the doctors this time.

I'm one of those types of people who asks "why" quite a lot. I'm a bit crazy like that. Why do children get glue ear? Why does the adenoid become enlarged? In our experience with health professionals, no one really cares and when you try and talk about it, you get nowhere.

'Why isn't there more focus on prevention rather than dealing with the symptoms?' I asked.

The Specialist looked at The Wife. The Wife looked at me.

'It's a valid question? I mean, it would prevent a lot of pain and anguish for all involved. Especially the kids.'

The Specialist placed a pen down and faced The Wife. Ignoring me.

'Mrs Glennon. Don't bring your husband again. He's annoying.'

Both boys had the procedures within a couple of months of one another. It made a massive difference to our family, but we'd co-slept from the beginning and somehow the boys needed to understand we no longer wanted their sweaty bodies anywhere near us during the night.

A new routine was required. A new bunkbed and a watertight plan. 5 pm teatime. 05:30 pm bath. 06:00 pm till 7 pm lowlights and chilled music.

Calm games.

Ove could have a bottle of oat milk, stories read, wees, complex questions concerning the nature of Cheerio's resolved. One parent kissed and squeezed. Two children in bed with classical music tinkering away, night light on and voila! It only went and flipping worked!

Kind of.

Mostly.

For a while.

I won't complain.

Getting them to sleep is a doddle now but getting them to stay asleep continues to be a massive pain in the arse.

Why Do They Always Shout?

'DAD, CAN YOU PLAY WITH ME?'

I glance at myself in the mirror: Pen on my face, questionable stains all over my t-shirt, tired red eyes, and one sock. I'm stood up but I can't feel my legs. I was on the way to the kitchen for something, I think, but I have no idea what for.

'COME ON, DAD. LET'S PLAY CARS.'

I'm holding a small fire engine. There're dozens of cars all around me on the floor like a minefield. There're homemade ramps leaning against every piece of furniture. Sections of wooden train track, which I was sure had been sent to the charity shop are now scattered in all directions.

Confusion.

'Haven't we been playing cars for the last... erm, is it daytime yet?'

'I WANNA WATCH THE SECRET LIFE OF PETS.'

'You just said you wanted to –'

'COME ON, DAD, LET'S WATCH THE SECRET LIFE OF PETS TWO.'

Why is he shouting at me? He's about half a metre away, standing on The Wife's exhausted body, giving him a few extra inches in height and sound range. He's naked and splattered with everything.

'Son, use your indoor voice, please.'

'I WANT SOMETHING TO EAT. GET ME SOMETHING.'

'Hmm, mmm, arrr, oooh.'

'What's that, Babe?'

The Wife pulls *Chase* from *Paw Patrol,* who looks like he's been mentally and physically abused, off her face.

'I said, why's he always shouting?'

'MUMMY! THERE YOU ARE. I COULDN'T FIND YOU.'

'I think there's something wrong with him,' I say.

'I WANNA WATCH THE SECRET LIFE OF PETS TWO.'

'I heard you, Son. Please stop shouting, you're gonna wake your brother up,' The Wife says.

There's a sudden thud above us. The Wife and I look up. Dust detaches itself from the light fitting and drifts along a beam of sunlight towards the crack in the curtain.

THUD THUD THUD down the stairs.

We stare at the door.

It opens. Slowly.

'MAMAAAAA,' Ove screams.

NOW THERE ARE TWO OF THEM!

The wild toddler with piercing blue eyes sniffs the air. He smells the last traces of milk inside The Wife's boob. He licks his lips. I've seen that look before. He won't be satisfied until he's drained her completely.

'MAMAAAAA.'

I crash through the minefield of cars, tracks, and ramps, and then army roll forward. I place *Chase* back on The Wife's face, muffling out the groans, then collect Arlo under one arm as I jump towards the dribbling toddler in the doorway, cutting off his boob attack before he formulates a plan of action.

I kick the kitchen door open and enter. A third arm smashes through my ribcage splattering the worktop with pieces of bone and dressing gown. This new arm instinctively knows what to do and stuffs chocolates, biscuits, and cartons of juice into their hands and into my pockets. I dive back through the kitchen door and head for the stairs.

'WHERE'S MY IPAD? I WANNA WATCH-'

He calls it an iPad but it's an Amazon Fire Tablet, but there's no point telling him that. He doesn't care! I throw them both up the

277

stairs with the exact amount of force required for a gentle landing then return to the kitchen.

'Where are they, where are they?'

'MAMAAAA,' Ove shouts.

'WHERE'S MY IPAD?' Arlo screams!

The tablets are charging next to the toaster. I plugged them in last night so they are ready to go!

'God is great!'

I grab the tablets off the side while my third arm unplugs them from their chargers, and I run. I run like I've never run before. The world is just a blur. My feet don't touch the floor. There is no floor. No time or space. My body ascends to a higher vibrational state where matter doesn't exist.

Again, my third arm works independently, interpreting my thoughts without hesitation and grabbing my *Game of Thrones* novel out of my coat pocket which hangs from the bannister. I ain't watching *Secret Life of Pets* ever again! No, no, no, and I ascend the stairs towards the boys who are regrouping their forces and starting to climb back down.

Not today boys!

In a flash, we're on their bed with the tablets in our hands, and snacks in our mouths.

'Today, you can watch all the films.'

'ALL THE FILMS?'

'Yes. And eat all the snacks.'

'ALL OF THEM?'

'Yes, all of them.'

'YAY,' they shout.

Seriously, why do they always shout?

A Lockdown Story

Lockdown has altered my perception of time, maaan. I have no idea what day it is, maaan. There's nothing concrete left in the world which says, today is Friday. Friday used to be the day I drink wine and eat crisps but now this is every day.

When I was a kid we bathed on a Sunday because school was the next day. As an adult, I showered after a day's work because it's what you do. It's routine. Unconscious routine.

But there is no school. NO work.

Only wine and crisps. And the kids, of course, but I haven't seen them for ages. They've blended into the sofa. I just throw food in their general direction and the cushions flap wildly for a few seconds then it all calms down. I return every so often to clean the scraps up off the floor.

I presume they're okay. The sofa hasn't told me any different.

It's an alternative reality, you see. Where all the rules and structures that usually keep me balanced in life have vanished. Have you ever thought, *I wish I could spend more time with my family?* No problem, mate. In this reality, your family is here, all the time. There aren't many places you can go to now. Once you've visited the same boring park over and over again, you eventually decide outside bad, inside good.

Everything you've ever wanted, sort of, is right here for you. A nice man delivers boxes of wine straight to your door. You play this really funny game where you put six bottles in the garage - they're for Christmas you tell yourself - and you put the other six in the kitchen - they're for the week ahead. The first six don't last long and the other six never judge when you appear at the garage door.

'I thought Christmas was a little ambitious if I'm honest,' Garage Wine says.

'Thanks for saying that. I thought so too.'

'Why don't you have a bottle with lunch?'

'What a wonderful idea.'

Just admit now, wine is better than water.

You get on first-name terms with hundreds of Amazon delivery drivers. They don't need to rush anymore. Everyone's in the house watching their brand-new Disney Plus subscription.

'Just leave it next to the bins if I'm not in, Alex,' you say for a laugh.

Alex smiles politely because he's heard it about twenty times already that morning and it wasn't funny the first time. He knows you aren't going anywhere. The Amazon drivers are living their best life and it would be even better if they could just shove it through your window and move on without having to listen to the drunken ramblings of all the parents desperate for a bit of adult conversation.

The supermarket trucks are the only other vehicles on the road. Those drivers don't have time to chat because they're so overwhelmed with orders. They supply large nets that you erect near your front door and they throw the shopping from the back of the trucks into it. And that's okay because in this reality you're a lazy slob and you don't want to come face-to-face with the person who's delivering your junk food and booze while you're wearing a dressing gown which looks like it was found in a skip.

Seriously, when was the last time I showered? I'm convinced that after a while my nose stops recognising the stench as an issue. Think out-of-date tin of corned beef mixed with a dash of garlic, a dollop of vinegar and a whole lot of parmesan cheese, and you're on the right track. Revolting to you, maybe? But to me, it has evolved into something quite pleasant. Kind of homely. Like homemade bread mixed with something earthy and dead.

The Wife's not said anything. And she's got a very sensitive nose, plus the inability to disguise the look of disgust on her face, so I can't be that bad.

Smell is subjective though isn't it? A fine example: I was ironing recently, and I thought to myself, this new washing powder's a bit funky. In fact, it's not very nice at all. But I carried on. The Wife likes to add white vinegar to everything, so I never know what is normal anymore. But one second after entering the room, The Wife says, "Cat piss?" And she was right.

Once she pointed it out, I was like, oh yeah. But she's said nothing about my new body odour so I'm going to continue with my homemade bready earthiness until things are back to normal. When Friday is for drinking wine and eating crisps, and Sunday is for having a bath!

Becca

It took me a while to figure it out, but you know what's harder than being a stepdad? Being a stepdaughter! I'm sorry it took so long to understand this. Probably could have made your life a bit easier in parts if I'd have known it sooner. This is not an excuse, but you need to know, to understand, that I was wildly unprepared for parenthood. In any form.

Especially when I was 29 years old!

I liked the simple things in life; going out drinking, having zero responsibility, eating white bread, avoiding close relationships, watching telly in bed whenever I liked and basically being accountable to no one. It was an easy life, and I was good at living it. I was the best at living my life.

I never expected to become a stepdad. I didn't see myself falling in love with your mum either, so really if you think about it, all roads lead back to her. She forced me to become a responsible adult when I wasn't ready!

It took me a while to understand the rules of parenting. Still learning. I was good at the easy stuff like going on holiday, theme parks and playing Mario Cart until my fingers went numb. I was great at facilitating lazy mornings with treats and films, spur-of-the-moment days out or trips to the cinema. It was easy when you were 10 years old. You were never demanding and, even though you'd had some shitty experiences as a kid, you were always up for a laugh and for the first four years I would say we laughed more than anything else.

It's when you became a fully-fledged teenager the wheels began to fall off!

Things got complicated and I could no longer figure out the right thing to do. Then when I did, I couldn't always tell you because you would give us the silent treatment for weeks on end. In many ways, I hated the silence much more than the arguing. It made me feel a bit lost. My man-brain could never find the right words to fix the problem which was very frustrating considering I pride myself on my problem-solving skills, and my ability to step back and analyse a situation.

Obviously not so good when it involves my own fuck ups!

Plus, it was doubly difficult for my problem-solving brain to compute that the issue was actually mine and not yours. I've had to dig deep to uncover the origin of these issues and I continue to develop my understanding of it all to ensure my reactions are balanced and calm (ish) while dealing with your brothers.

I dread to think what they're going to be like as teenagers!

Yep, it's fair to say we've changed a lot, haven't we? It's been over a decade since we became a family and we've shared the ups and downs, trials and tribulations of life. I think we've all come out the other side stronger and wiser.

But getting to this point of understanding has been difficult and I want to say, I'm sorry. I'm sorry for the times when you've felt like you had nowhere to go. When you didn't feel welcome in your own home. When good days were turned to shit and you were scared of what I might say next or what mood I was in.

I'm not suggesting you were an innocent little saint in all of this of course but you deserved my gentler side more often.

I am truly sorry.

But I can't take it back.

I can't say I wish things would've been different because without the drama I wouldn't have learnt so much about myself. Without flushing out so many negative aspects of my personality I wouldn't be the dad I am today, and your brothers wouldn't be benefiting from the person you've helped create.

So, thank you for that. Because you were a flipping walk in the park compared to these two sleep thieves and I can't see how I would've coped with these two ten years ago.

Cold breeze... shudder.

I believe things happen for a reason and you are clearly strong enough to handle almost anything. More than you give yourself credit for. Lessons come from the strangest of places sometimes and I'm happy to admit, you've been one of my greatest teachers.

Thank you. I love you. I owe you a drink.

You've had to endure parts of me which were angry and scrambling to control everything, and you've come out the other side amazingly.

I'm going to take 40%, minimum, responsibility for your amazingness.

I've always told you things straight. As I see them anyway. Your mum might say sometimes a little too plainly but my openness meant you came to me with issues which you didn't want to discuss with your mum. You've always talked to me about your life or concerns, knowing I wouldn't bullshit you or try and tell you what to do.

Sort of.

I might have subtly coerced you a few times, but it was always for your own good!

Can I ask, have you forgiven me for the whole Father Christmas debacle or is that still a bit raw? I'm not actually sorry about that. Sorry.

I saved you from looking like a right div in secondary school. Believe me. Anyways, thanks for sticking by me.

Those brothers of yours take so much from your mum and I, as you know, and I truly hope that hasn't made you feel pushed out. That you're not loved equally.

Because you are.

The great thing is you don't need us like you once did. You're super independent and rocking it on your career path but please know, we are here for you. If you need us, for anything, let us know. Don't think you're so grown up that you can't call us just for a good whinge. Okay?

I love you. I still haven't received that £100 by the way... give me £100!

Jack and the Beanstalk

On reflection, going to the pantomime to watch *Jack and the Beanstalk* on Boxing Day, the day after consuming a year's supply of Ferrero Rocher, was probably not the best idea.

'You're going to love it,' said The Wife.

'Oh no I won't.'

'Oh yes you will!'

'Oh no I...'

I was right. It was stressful. Taking small children to any enclosed space where other humans gather sends a cold shiver down my spine at the best of times. Never mind an enclosed space surrounded by like-minded little beasts. All waving around battery-powered nunchucks with repeating flashing lights able to produce a hypnotic state a split second before cracking you in the teeth!

'It'll be great. They'll love it,' The Wife assured me.

My brain can, and often does, replay HD video evidence from the last time, every time, when they've been taken somewhere where

"They'll love it." It always ends the same way, either attempting to manage their behaviour peacefully by talking to them like civil human beings or resorting to bribery. I find it much easier to just pretend they're not mine.

Why would this day be any different? Where does The Wife draw her unshakeable faith from?

I'm a realist. I knew exactly how it was going to go.

At the Stockport Plaza on Boxing Day 2019, Ove, then two, was on glorious form. He took it upon himself to act out his own performance – one filled with uncontrollable bouts of screaming and contortionism.

Each attempt to keep him seated saw every muscle in his little body completely relax and he would flop through my grasp and head under the seats towards the exit.
Always towards the exit.

Which told me something about how much he was loving it. He was like me. We would rather have been at home supping from a bottle of something nice with one hand and stroking our stuffed bellies with the other while watching a film.

Arlo, aged four and occasionally able to sit still for longer than ten minutes, was enthralled. No bother at all. Unlike his brother. By the halfway point it was obvious we weren't going to make it through the second half in one piece.

At times like this when elbowing the popcorn out of the hands of those sitting to my right, blocking the stage from those behind, while passing a toddler back and forth between us every minute, I couldn't help but consider if it all would have been better if I was slightly tipsy. But I'd made the suggestion on the way, it felt so righteous at the time, that I wouldn't drink alcohol.

Why? Because I'm stupid.

But my brain repeatedly forced me to look at the back of the theatre to the bar where people were getting refreshments before the second half began.

Mind: Go and get a beer.

Me: No.

Mind: You deserve it.

Me: I said I wouldn't.

Mind: You're allowed to change your mind.

Me: Don't say that.

Mind: Look at that dad over there.

I turned to see a fellow dad with two small children who were sitting on either side of him. They were eating chocolate, casually chatting, and waiting patiently while dad sipped on a cold pint. I caught his eye as he dipped into his super-sized bag of chilli Doritos, washed down with a long gulp from his plastic cup of freezing cold yellow loveliness.

Mind: You want to be that guy.

Me: He's my hero.

I looked beyond that lucky bastard and noticed some empty seats tucked away where the buggies were stored.

We're having those seats!

I immediately sprang into action.

'Where are you going?' The Wife hissed.

Her eyes were watery and wide – she touched my arm and psychically pleaded with me not to leave her alone.

'I have a plan,' I reassured her.

She grasped my wrist so tight I was transported back to primary school when a teacher dragged me along the corridor to the head's office.

'I'll be back in a minute.'

I peeled off one clamped finger at a time then slid out of the cramped seating row like a Ninja towards the Steward who was helping a granny sit down.

'Hi mate. You need to help me. Please.'

'I'll see what I can do.'

'I have two wild kids, one of them may or may not have incarnated in human form to test our physical and mental endurance, but long story short, we need those seats at the back out of the way please.'

He glanced over.

'I'm not sure. It's for wheelchair users.'

'Totally get that, but I've noticed it's not being used today.'

'I'll speak to my supervisor.'

I nodded and stuck to him like glue as he found a grey-haired lovely-faced lady standing at an exit, keeping her wise eyes on the crowd. He whispered into her ear and she peered into my soul, recognising a genuine need for help. Plus, I was on my knees with hands clasped together in prayer, shaking them furiously!

She nodded like a pro.

I told her I owed her one and flew down the aisle towards my family. The Wife was holding Ove between her hands as he twisted from side to side and kicked her repeatably in the chest, like a fish with legs, while spinning the fluorescent front teeth remover above his head.

'Right you three, come on.'

The Wife didn't ask anything. We could've been going home at that point and she wouldn't have argued. She threw both kids through the air one at a time and I placed them against the wall and pinned them there with a foot. The Wife whispered apologies to those collecting teeth off the floor and met me on the aisle.

'What's going on?' she asked.

'Follow me.'

I picked both boys up and walked with purpose past those returning to their seats as the lights were dimmed and the show resumed. The Wife followed, confused, without saying a word. When we arrived at the cordoned-off area, the Steward was waiting for us. He removed the rope and waved us to our new private seating area. The kids scrambled out of my arms and immediately got themselves comfy in their own large seats with a clear view of the stage.

The Wife hugged the Steward, and I shook his hand vigorously.

The Wife and I made several pleasant sounds as we lowered our battered bodies into the spacious seats. She gave me a look which suggested marrying me was the best thing she'd ever done and if I never accomplished anything else of meaning in my life again, this was enough.

The rest of the show was incident free. Pantomime is not my go-to theatrical form of entertainment, but I appreciate the appeal. It's more relaxed than a regular theatre experience. *Jack and the Beanstalk* was fun, festive, and energised, but the Boxing Day blues seemed to have affected most of the crowd. For a theatrical genre that requires, and greatly benefits from audience participation, my heart went out to the performers.

To say the mood was a little flat would be the understatement of the century. I hadn't noticed during the first half because my whole focus was on Ove's escape plans.

It was a tough slog for the performers. Jokes, musical numbers, and choreographed routines which might have been enthusiastically applauded on other nights, were met with mild slapping sounds and grunts of interest.

Imagine, you've been steadily grazing on pickles, nuts, crisps, and savoury things dipped in cheese all day - you've consumed copious amounts of new and exciting chocolates.

You've had your Christmas dinner, probably second helpings and pudding. Maybe some cheese and crackers as well. You honestly can't imagine eating anything else for days.

Then someone asks if you want another mince pie?

No.

You didn't have one when you were peckish and tipsy from Bucks Fizz so why would you want one now while bloated and disgusting? You don't. But the inevitable happens.

You turn your puffy head ever so slightly to the side and flick an acknowledgement of interest with your forehead while grunting.

That's what the audience response was like.

Even the cheeky scouser playing Simple Simon, who had the best lines and freedom to improvise had to dig deep to drag a response from the lacklustre crowd. I'm not one for public displays of enthusiasm but I felt obliged to raise my game and applaud, jeer, and boooooo in order to contribute to the show. Whereas in truth, I would usually nod and clap in the right places like a good dad. But not this night. I was right up there with The Wife.

"He's behind you."

"Oh no he's not."

Booing the bad guy, clapping, laughing loudly, all that shit. I honestly didn't think I had it in me.

At the end I looked down at the dad with his empty plastic cup, planning his escape route through the mass of bodies, wild-eyed sugar fuelled kids, and neglectful parents slinging baby-changing bags over their shoulders. Our eyes met. How quickly roles can be reversed ay mate? I didn't gloat. Didn't have the time because we removed the rope from our VIP area and walked, unmolested, straight out the door and into the crisp December night.

We strolled home with Ove strapped in the buggy while Arlo stood on the buggy board and retold the whole *Jack and the Beanstalk* story to us. The Wife and I nodded and responded cheerily when required. Occasionally we looked into each other's eyes and passed those unspoken words between us as we approached our home.

Never again.

But we will. We always do!

They Win

They win. They're the champions. They've won the battle and the war. We've been beaten so mercilessly that I honestly don't know why we didn't wave the white flag years ago. Life could've been soooo much easier if we had done.

Congratulations you little sleep thieves!

I don't even feel bad about it. I'm glad they won. They've put so much effort into playing the game that it would've been a pity for them to lose in the end. The only real shame is they have no idea they were even playing in the first place.

At least they can't be smug about it.

It's all so clear now, here at the end. Defeated. Relieved. I can look back at all the pain and suffering of war, the fatigued bodies limping towards the kitchen for the tenth cup of tea before 10 am, dressed in dirty rags, red-eyed and unable to remember which white box was for dishes and which one was for rags, and I see how pointless it all was.

That's the painful bit – hindsight – looking back at what could have been if we'd only understood we were fighting a losing battle.

Actually, I do feel bad.

Bad for The Wife and I who've been participating in a war we were ill-equipped to fight!

Many moons ago, when I could venture out after dark wearing nice clothes and aftershave, I played poker at a pub. I'd never really played before, but I had a general idea of what to do. *Real* poker enthusiasts, people who have invested time and energy into their craft, hate playing against people like me.

I wasn't following a strategy or thinking about the other person's hand. I was working off Guinness, luck and a naïve intuition about my own hand which worked amazingly and got me a seat in the final where it all unravelled terribly because I was eight pints in and thinking more about the jukebox than the game.

But was I bothered? Not at all. I'd knocked several well-seasoned players out of the game and I didn't really know how I was doing it.

'Two pairs, Kings and Jacks,' Seasoned Player said.

He placed his cards on the table. Chuffed.

'Argh, you got me,' I said. 'Two pairs as well but I only have tens. I was close though.'

His knuckles turned white.

'You have a Full House.'

'Is that good?' I inquired.

I think he went straight home to bed.

You see, the players were stressing and getting annoyed, and I was just enjoying myself, drinking Guinness, munching crisps, going for a smoke, and playing my favourite tunes on the jukebox. It was a great night. There was nothing these experienced players could do to stop me because, like my boys, I wasn't emotionally connected to the outcome. I was just living my life, placing cards on a table, and hoping for the best. The outcome didn't really matter because I was enjoying all the aspects of the evening.

Now I know how it must have felt for them; to be playing against an ignorant person (and I mean that in its truest sense, a person with a lack of knowledge) and think you can somehow come out on top just because you have more experience - because you have the knowledge. Ha. It doesn't always work out like that I'm afraid because when you're playing against two agenda-less sleep thieves your past experiences aren't worth a damn.

My boys won. They cleared up. Royal flush!

What have they won exactly? Our adult time. The Wife and I now have zero evening time together. We give up. It's pointless. We're in bed at 8 pm at the latest. Earlier most days.

Do you remember being a kid and complaining to your parents about going to bed while it was still sunny outside? I'm not going to do that because we accept that we will not sleep, ever again, past 5 am. Bed for 8 pm with the very real chance of getting to sleep for 9 pm which actually gives us eight, mainly undisturbed, hours' sleep.

It's the best we've had it in six years. Why am I not thrilled with this prospect? I should be buzzing! I'll tell you why I'm not. It's a well-known fact that nothing exciting, in the whole of human history, has ever happened to people who go to bed before 8 pm.

Nothing... Ever! It never has and never will.

Well, maybe one small thing. Going to bed earlier means it's acceptable to open a bottle of wine earlier. 4 pm to be exact. This means wine with tea which I've been advocating for ages. The Wife has been strictly against it since the whole brush with alcoholism fiasco during the first lockdown, and because putting the kids to bed after consuming wine makes her sleepy. She still sits with them until they fall asleep.

Cute.

Me? I take the boys to bed, speed-read through two books, kiss them both, turn the light off, say goodnight and shut the door.

Job done in fifteen minutes whereas it once took hours.

So you know what? I was feeling defeated but it's clear now we're all winners here. This is a shared victory. Going to bed at 8 pm is cool and I'm very happy about it.

Did that sound convincing to you? I almost believed it myself.

Being Dad

He thinks it's an identity crisis. Sort of. Although the word crisis doesn't fit because he likes it. It feels good. He was once so sure of who he was and what he liked but the memory of that guy is rapidly fading. He gets caught off guard. He might be brushing his teeth, opening a bottle of wine, or lying in the dark hoping that was the cat who just thudded in the other room at 4 am and not one of his boys getting up.

In those off-guard moments, a not-so-exciting image from the past POPS into his mind's eye suddenly. He watches it, confused, "Why is my brain showing me this?" then continues to observe as it develops into a little movie in his head where he's cooking spaghetti bolognese in a grubby kitchen where he lived years ago. He even had hair!

An all-knowing sense of what else happened on that utterly normal evening will merge with the movie in his head. The music playing - he can't hear it but knows it's there - is probably one of the mixed CDs he used to make regularly. He's swigging red wine from a half-pint glass.

How uncouth.

He's halfway through the first bottle, and a second will be finished; one was never enough. He'll smoke a couple of roll-ups like he always did when having a drink and, without fail, he'll spend most of the evening watching films and texting several different female acquaintances. Social media hadn't taken over back then. Simpler days.

That young man was passionate about things. Full of energy, anger, and love! There was a fire in his belly that pushed him to get things done without overcomplicating the idea. He knows the image of the young man is from his twenties and rationally he's aware of the traits of a young man at that age, but why this image? Why now?

Is he supposed to acknowledge that there's a part of himself which has gone and will never return? Has the fire gone? Did it burn out or was it taken away?

Now life needs a plan. He can't just have an idea and pursue it 24/7 until satisfied. Passion has been replaced with a dream board filled with images, dates, and cheesy motivational phrases.

"A dream is just a goal without a plan." "Be your authentic self." "You're worthy of success."

He looks at that dusty dream board. How did he get to the point where pursuing an idea needed visualising on a piece of card?

Gradually he began replacing his hobbies, wants, passions, dreams, youth, desires, friendships, social life, career, all-day drink and drug sessions, gigs, doing fack all, personal hygiene, personal development, putting sugar in tea, eating microwave pizza and chips, watching all three Lord of the Rings special edition box sets in bed just because he had a hint of a cold, with the wants and needs of his family.

Is that just the way it goes? Does it have to be like that?

All those things are now a series of blended images in his mind that no longer fit coherently together. Like a damaged jigsaw. Some of the pieces have been chewed around the edges. They're soggy. Others have faded.

He can look at the image on a piece and know what it's supposed to be – he can see a person who looks like him standing with some other people, who he kind of recognises, in a place he's sure he's been, but he just can't place himself there anymore. It's just floating around in the jigsaw of his mind, existing but without a place. No context.

After experiencing all this madness in his mind, he returns to the present with another word in mind, gratitude. He wouldn't be anywhere else in the world if you paid him. He doesn't want to be that guy cooking in the kitchen alone.

His life was hard. Full of unexpected challenges which occasionally broke him and left him deflated.

Everything was fought hard for and easily lost. The desire to live at a hundred miles per hour, jam-packing in as many sensory experiences as possible, has matured into a quality-over-quantity kind of attitude.

Watching his boys live their lives gives him a much deeper pleasure than he knew possible. Sharing a bottle of wine with his wife, allowing her to win at cards while discussing their present, is significantly more satisfying than the fly-by-night relationships from the past.

If the only two jobs he did well in this life were being a good dad and a loving husband, he'd be happy with that. And grateful for the opportunity.

Mums of the World,
I Get it Now!

It's hard work being a parent, someone should be paying us to do it. I'm not joking. Without the kids of the now, who'll be the adults of the future? And if our sleep-deprived brains finally slide out of the dish, who's going to care for them? I have a vision of social services knocking on the door.

'Hello, Mr Glennon, we've come to check on you and your partner. We've had reports your children are attempting to push you into a catatonic state?'

'Yhnnsn beeeeeee.'

'Yes, milk and two sugars please.'

'Hhgeee beeeeya.'

'Soya milk's fine.'

I wave her inside and she follows me into the lounge where the children are hanging upside down from rope swings attached to the ceiling. They're both naked and filthy. Smeared with the remnants of food and messy play. Wide-eyed and alert. Chewing slowly on something fruit-like and sticky.

The Wife's sitting at the table facing the window.

'Mmnnhxh knjcsnsjj,' I say.

'Okay, Babe,' The Wife replies without turning.

I go off to the kitchen to make the brews.

'How long has he been talking like that?'

'Three weeks now. I couldn't understand him at first. I had to tune in.'

'It's very common for new Dads. Especially ones who survived the nineteen nineties. They don't have many brain cells left to begin with and parenthood, well, it can easily take the rest.'

'Taggy waggy woooo... ahem. Sorry.'

The Wife wraps her arms tightly around herself and begins to rock gently.

'I can see you're in the very early stages too, Mrs Glennon. How long's it been happening?'

'This morning at 04:52 am when the boys decided it was time to turn their bedroom into a den. They needed all our covers and cushions apparently. I think I was trying to say get out of our room but instead, I blurted out, "Taggy waggy woooo."'

'Does Mr Glennon know?'

The Wife laughs hysterically. Her head swings wildly from side to side. She stamps her feet against the laminate floor.

'Mrs Glennon?'

The Wife stops instantly.

'Does Mr Glennon know, you ask?'

I step into the lounge with a large tray which I place on the dining table next to The Wife. The social worker steps forward and gasps in horror but recovers her composure quickly. I pass a miniature Sylvanian Family teacup to The Wife and one to the social worker who accepts it with great care as if it contains a hot liquid.

She even gives it a little blow.

'Thanks.'

'Taggy waggy woooo,' I tell her.

The Wife turns in her chair.

'Taggy waggy wooo,' The Wife says.

'Taggy waggy wooo,' both the boys say.

They drop to the floor, landing directly on their heads, then get up, completely unaffected, and walk slowly towards the social worker. They continue ripping large chunks from an unidentified red fruit. The social worker places the miniature teacup back on the tray and begins a slow but purposeful retreat towards the hallway and eventual freedom.

'Someone from my office will be in touch,' she says before gently closing the front door behind her.

We all stand at the window and wave her off whilst sipping from our miniature teacups.

I think £30,000 per year to be a parent sounds about fair. I've had numerous jobs throughout my life, and none are as demanding as being a domesticated stay-at-home dad. And to all the mums who have been doing it from day one, you deserve some kind of back payment. A damages cheque in the post. Recognition for services to humanity or something.

To all the mums, I salute you. And apologise on behalf of all the unappreciative kids and husbands out there. We didn't know!

We didn't know you had to put in a wash every day. That not all items of clothing can go in the dryer. We didn't know there wasn't a magical way to pair socks or get the creases out of jeans without ironing them. It never occurred to us that you might want some time off for yourself.

We thought you liked doing everything. We just didn't know. We couldn't see past our own needs.

Again, I'm sorry.

But I know now, oh how I know now!

I've broken through the veil of ignorance. I see you now. I know your pain. We're in this together. When I see the occasional parent outside the nursery in the morning, smartly dressed, fresh-faced and composed, I think, who are these freaks of nature? What's their secret? I want to tug at their sleeve, whisper into their ear, "How do you do it? You look so clean."

But as the urge to speak merges with my ability to register the idea, I realise I'm standing with the car fob in my hand staring at an old man in the reflection of the car window. He resembles me, slightly. I recognise those tired red eyes but there's an unidentified brown smear on his left cheek and he looks broken – close to tears.

How many days straight has he worn that t-shirt? Does he know it's tucked into his back-to-front boxer shorts?

Is that really me?

I'm going to go out on a limb and say outright that some parents have it harder than others but if you've been away for the weekend without your kids while they're still under three, you guys don't have a flipping clue.
I used to smile a lot, and wear skinny jeans, and a variety of funky-looking shoes. Now I live in shorts and hoodies, splattered

313

with porridge and jam, but at least it's organic, ha, ha, ha, ha, ha, sniffle, sniffle, sob, sob.

Seriously how did it come to this?

The kids are always poorly, and they don't sleep. When I hear a parent say, "Oh, little Joshy had me up all night, he didn't go to sleep till 8 pm and woke up at 6 am, I'm exhausted."

My eye twitches and I want to grab that parent by the shoulders and shake them violently while screaming in their face, "You have no idea!" before falling at their feet sobbing, begging them to let me sleep at their house for a night.

At its worst, when Arlo was a baby, he would sleep for fifty minutes and scream for twenty. That was almost every night for two and a half years before he was diagnosed with glue ear. It nearly broke us.

Now, he only wakes once or twice a night. Manageable. Ove however, one year old, also suffering from glue ear, wakes about six times a night but he only cries and doesn't scream, ha, ha, ha, ha, ha, sniffle, sniffle, sob, sob.

Seriously how did it come to this?

I know we aren't the only ones suffering with this job. I see those freaks of nature parents looking fresh-faced and organised, and I know it's fakery. They've probably had a couple of good nights sleep and got a bit giddy and thought, "You know what, I'm going to have a shower and put clean clothes on!"

Fakery!

I mainly interact with the other parents. The ones like me; the confused, the lethargic. They walk the supermarket aisles with upside-down shopping lists looking for foods they would never have bought five years ago. We walk past one another, a knowing look is exchanged, words aren't necessary.

We both know what this day is. Nursery day! I adjust the shopping list for her, and she wipes the crumbs from my shoulder. We force a smile and continue along our way.

We should be paid for this job!

"No one asked you to have kids," I hear some of you say.

That's not true. The Wife did.

When calculating our financial worth as a parent: Combine our daily cleaning chores, dealing with the tricksy washing basket (which makes you question reality because it's impossible to empty completely) with the constant detective work required to locate all the discarded food and spiky toys on the floor. Add childcare, medical services, emotional support, human punchbag and hourly comedic performances and I'm sure we'd be worth £60,000 per year but I'm a realist. I'd happily settle for £30,000 to develop two compassionate, empathic adults of the future.

To My Boys

Hello Boys. I really hope I'm not in a mental institute while you're reading these words but anything's possible. I could be dead! If that's the case make sure your mum has erected a shrine to my greatness somewhere in the house. It doesn't have to be the front room. I'd be happy with the kitchen where I've spent most of my life since your mum decided she can only make jacket potato and beans.

But it's unlikely I've met with an untimely demise because, despite your best efforts to cripple us both mentally through a relentless, and I mean this Boys, your relentless attack on our basic human right to sleep longer than four hours, I'm in pretty good shape. Your Mum? She's currently walking around in circles looking for her sanity after a particularly early rise of 04:50 am caused by you Ove G. She's got to get ready for work soon and attempt to act normal for the day. I don't know how she does it.

You two have no idea.

We protect you from the despair by pushing through and finding a way to cope. I'm currently researching the legality of placing bolts on both of your doors because I'm a doer!
It's lucky you're both cute.

Ove, you recently turned three. You are obsessed with toy fighting and weapons. I have a cut on my head where you cracked me on the head with a wooden sword yesterday. Fanks. You also love lying down twiddling our nipples to the point of scabbing while sipping on a fine oat milk. You're still finding your voice but the language you've created is beautiful and we understand most of it.

Lockdown March 2020 came at a key stage in your personal development. This was prime learning and socialising time and unfortunately, it took those opportunities away from you. But you're very happy and we're trying our best to support you the best we can while you figure out what you like to do and what your interests are.

Arlo, you're (in your own words) five and a half and three-quarters. You love making up stories and songs which you soothe Ove with in the middle of the night after I've plonked him back in his own bed. Your stories are fantastical and funny. You merge your personal experiences with other stories and songs you've heard with great skill. You're a very gentle person who loves being around other people.

You regularly congratulate strangers for their choice of hair colour, fashion sense, or anything else that springs to your mind. This always brings a smile to even the grumpiest of faces. You bring so much laughter into the world, Boys, and I'm 100% accurate in saying this, you get your humour from me.

Ha-ha Wife, write your own book.

Oh, but you both love a good kick-off too.

Snacks and technology are the sources of most of these eruptions. There Are several ways we manage this. Good old-fashioned "no." Your mum's favourite. I tend to lean on the classics like hide and seek or other physical games because, fundamentally, you both love playing more than anything else. You just don't know that yet.

Sometimes, me and your mum are too tired to play because (read the rest of the book to find out all the details) sleep deprivation has pushed us to the very limit of human endurance and every so often all we have to offer is our unconditional love, chocolate, and bubbles.

But the crazy thing is I wouldn't change anything. Life is what it is, Boys. Living with two sleep thieves has also pushed us towards positive things: Self-development, reflection, endurance, and love.

The desire to relinquish old wounds and behaviours underpinned by our own traumas which laid the groundwork for our personalities, fears, quirks, biases, addictions, anger management skills, or lack of.

Basically, I won't apologise for snapping now and again and you don't have to apologise for nearly killing us through sleep deprivation. Deal? Cool.

Things have changed a lot.

It's just the four of us now since moving to Devon, leaving Becca behind in Stockport. That was a huge decision. Not one we ever expected to make. A proper fork-in-the-road moment for us all.

It came down to several factors and one being she didn't need us as much as she once did. She's a young woman now and we wouldn't have entertained the idea of moving unless we believed 100% in Becca's ability to handle it.

Probably 80-85% to be honest.

It's tough sometimes because we don't have anyone else here with us. We're still trying to utilise video calls to Granny and Grandpa, and Nana and Grandad. It's not the same of course and we know that. But it was part of the sacrifice we had to make because we were, and continue to be, convinced that it was important to offer you both something different.

We want you to have experiences that we never had.

This wasn't a completely selfless act. We wanted new and exciting opportunities for ourselves as well. But this period of our lives is also filled with external challenges that are preventing us from having a well-balanced mixture of experiences that humans deserve to have.

We disapprove of the lockdowns in all forms but here in our home, we focus on the positives and we shield ourselves from the fear-based media which portrays a bleak existence for us all.

In truth, this world is pretty amazing and most of the people you'll meet are as well.

In my emerging view, people must elevate themselves above fear and look inside. Feel their emotions and heal their psychological wounds. And outwardly it would be helpful if the world got rid of the elite ruling class, human trafficking, carcinogens from food and water, glitter, hourly news updates on the radio, and porn has probably got to go.

Having loads of different device chargers is an absolute waste of time. Updating software is another. World hunger has always been a problem.

How's it looking now?

Has amazing technology changed everything for the better? Or has AI enslaved humans and forced us all to live as one nation? No more wars or borders? Healthy living and no recreational drugs? A perfect balance of work, rest, and obedience? Sounds a bit boring to me.

Life is risk, Boys, and sometimes you get hurt.

Your mum and I can't control those things, so we concentrate on being the best we can be. When you read this for the first time, hopefully, we're still fully alive and kicking, and working hard together to give you and ourselves the best life we can.

But seriously, technology is an issue. Arlo, you like to ask, "Can I have my iPad," until you've bombarded my subconscious so profoundly, I begin to think it's my idea and give in. Arlo, just so you know, it's an Amazon Fire Tablet, not an iPad. Ove G, you like to rock in from nursery and point and scream at the telly until I put it on. I can dissuade you for a few minutes with a snack, you're just getting into puzzles, or by chasing you around the house like a madman for a few minutes but all roads lead back to finger-pointing and screaming at the telly.

Just so you know, we're gathering our strength and the winds of change are coming!

A combination of Lockdown restrictions and the winter weather has contributed towards more time indoors and an overreliance on devices. But spring is in the air and I'm hopeful for the lighter days ahead.

Technology has its place but there must be a way to introduce a healthy balance between screen time and playtime. When I was young computers were in their infancy. The options on the telly were limited and you pretty much had to watch whatever the oldest person in the room wanted to.

You boys get a lot of freedom and I just want you both to know now, if the screaming and shouting continue, I will sell every device in the house and move us into a caravan.

Maybe you're reading this now from that caravan with a mullet haircut and dodgy teeth?

Here's the inside scoop Boys; we don't know what we're doing! It's tough. As adults, we juggle much more than you know. Everything is free for you both and it's our job, the best job in the world, to make sure you have the things you need, within reason, and you feel loved and secure. I think we do a pretty good job at that.

Any complaints? Take it up with your social worker.

At the minute, Ove, you won't even entertain the thought of riding your little blue balance bike. When you didn't have one, all you wanted to do was try and have a go on other children's bikes. Now you have your own, do you care? Not at all. And that's fine, Son.

We are here to facilitate your interests as long as it's not eating pebbles or nipple twiddling. I hope you can ride your bike because I know it's lots of fun but maybe it's not like that for you right now.

Maybe you feel out of control?

If I had to choose between swimming and riding a bike though, I'll take swimming any day, Son. That's a natural life skill we all should acquire. You can't cycle away from a jellyfish.

It's tough for you at the moment, Arlo, because you're not getting a lot of time for independent play at home. Yes, we run around the house inventing games and setting traps but finding some alone time with your own thoughts has become more difficult. And that difficulty is also your best friend; Ove G.

Just when you've set everything up, world-building with blocks to the left, and a battered selection of cars scattered to the right, Ove G comes along and destroys it!

It's 100% his favourite thing to do.

We can't stop him, Son.

He's relentless in his quest to destroy your independent play. Sorry about that. But if it makes you feel any better, just know you're his favourite person in the world and he loves you incredibly.

This book is basically dedicated to you both. Without documenting our experiences in a way that hopefully brings a smile to people's faces, I would never have learnt so much about myself and my potential as a parent.

So nice one. Thanks.

But I want you to know that very soon your mum and I will be going away for a long weekend, and guess what... four's a crowd.

Not sure how it's going to manifest yet, but I see cold drinks in the evening sun, beautiful sea views and quiet time. Holding your mum's hand as we smile at one another, knowing you two lovely boys are sleeping somewhere familiar with people that love you.

Or at least like you enough to let you sleep over.

I'm not going to lie; we aren't as fussy as we used to be.

Anyway... thank you Arlo and Ove. Thanks for teaching me so much about myself. Thanks for bringing us so much joy and love. Thanks for all of it. And if by any chance I do find my way into a mental institute, tell them I like trippy drugs. Stronger the better.

Cheers, Boys.

WHY DO THEY ALWAYS SHOUT?

Conversations With a Kid

'Hi, Dad.'

'Hello, Son.'

'Did you have a good day at work?'

'It was alright. Nothing special.'

'Maybe you should get another job?'

'When you're a bit older maybe.'

'You'll be dead then.'

'Cheers, Son.'

The End

For now!

Printed in Great Britain
by Amazon

12177888R00190